One Day at a Time
A Self-Care Journal

A Product of

ONE DAY AT A TIME: A Self-Care Journal

One Day at a Time: A Self-Care Journal

Making a commitment to take better care of yourself is easy. Keeping the commitment, following through and maintaining forward progress is sometimes a little more difficult.

This journal is for anyone, at any stage of self-care. If you're making a new commitment to do something different than you've been doing, this journal allows you to take it step by step, day by day, and track only what you're doing today. You can look back and see progress and successes if you want to, but your goals are set each day, for that day only.

If you're in the midst of an ongoing commitment, great. This journal can help you as well. Write down what you've done, what you're doing, and keep a daily record of your commitment.

If you don't succeed one day, or don't do as much as you had hoped, it's only one day. The next morning, start up with new commitment and a brand new journal page, and try again.

Make it a goal to truly care about yourself, every single day.

ONE DAY AT A TIME: A Self-Care Journal

Disclaimer

Questions presented in the Journal are presented solely for the purpose of inspiring the reader to journal about his or her own goals and commitments. This journal should not be used to diagnose or prescribe treatment for any illness or disorder for a particular individual. It is not intended to replace the advice of doctors, nutritionists, psychiatrists, psychologists, therapists, physicians or health care practitioners and should not be used in place of a visit, call or consultation or the advice of a qualified care provider. The journal in no way provides medical or counseling advice. If, after working in this journal, you feel that you need help with a particular topic or area, we recommend seeking professional guidance and care from a qualified practitioner.

This journal, the author, and sponsoring company and publisher make no claim, guarantee or warranty as to the results that may be obtained from using the journal. The Journal, nor any of its authors, contributors, or other representatives will be liable for damages arising out of or in connection with the use of the journal. This applies to all damages of any kind, including (without limitation) compensatory, direct, indirect or consequential damages, loss of data, income or profit, loss of or damage to property and claims of third parties. Your use of the Journal confirms your agreement of the terms and conditions described herein. If you do not agree, you will not utilize the Journal.

Contacting Corporate Elements, LLC
If you have any questions about this document, please contact:

Amy S. Morgan
Corporate Elements, LLC
Amy@CorpElements.com
www.CorpElements.com
Phone (405) 326-4116

ONE DAY AT A TIME: A Self-Care Journal

Other Books by DoodlyCouch:

Doodle your feelings.

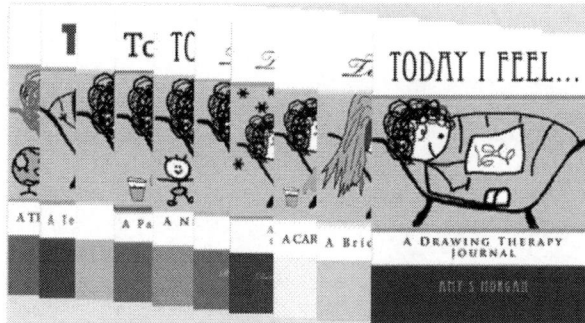

ONE DAY AT A TIME: A Self-Care Journal

ONE DAY AT A TIME: A Self-Care Journal

DATE:_____

Today I promise not to:_____

Today I promise to:_____

Today's Nutrition (circle 1 for each serving you have today):

Veggies:	1	2	3	4	5	6	7	8	9	10	11
Fruit:	1	2	3	4	5	6	7	8	9	10	11
Bread/Starch:	1	2	3	4	5	6	7	8	9	10	11
Dairy:	1	2	3	4	5	6	7	8	9	10	11
Protein:	1	2	3	4	5	6	7	8	9	10	11
Fats, Oils & Sweets	1	2	3	4	5	6	7	8	9	10	
Water:	1	2	3	4	5	6	7	8	9	10	11

Today's Fitness (enter #'s and types that fit your daily routine):

_____ Reps of _____   _____ Reps of_____

_____ Reps of _____   _____ Reps of_____

_____ Reps of _____   _____ Reps of_____

Other:_____

Other:_____

Money I Spent Today:

$_____ for _____ In my budget?   Yes   No

$_____ for _____ In my budget?   Yes   No

$_____ for _____ In my budget?   Yes   No

Something I Cleaned today:_____

Positive Interactions today:_____

_____

What I did towards Spiritual Growth today:_____

Today my biggest Personal Success was:_____

What I did for Someone Else today:_____

Today I am Grateful for:_____

Today I Feel:_____

Today I Learned:_____

Today I treated myself with love and care: Yes   No

ONE DAY AT A TIME: A Self-Care Journal

DATE:_____

Today I promise not to:_____

Today I promise to:_____

Today's Nutrition (circle 1 for each serving you have today):

Veggies:	1	2	3	4	5	6	7	8	9	10	11
Fruit:	1	2	3	4	5	6	7	8	9	10	11
Bread/Starch:	1	2	3	4	5	6	7	8	9	10	11
Dairy:	1	2	3	4	5	6	7	8	9	10	11
Protein:	1	2	3	4	5	6	7	8	9	10	11
Fats, Oils & Sweets	1	2	3	4	5	6	7	8	9	10	
Water:	1	2	3	4	5	6	7	8	9	10	11

Today's Fitness (enter #'s and types that fit your daily routine):

_____ Reps of _____   _____ Reps of_____

_____ Reps of _____   _____ Reps of_____

_____ Reps of _____   _____ Reps of_____

Other:_____

Other:_____

Money I Spent Today:

$_____ for _____ In my budget?   Yes   No

$_____ for _____ In my budget?   Yes   No

$_____ for _____ In my budget?   Yes   No

Something I Cleaned today:_____

Positive Interactions today:_____

_____

What I did towards Spiritual Growth today:_____

Today my biggest Personal Success was:_____

What I did for Someone Else today:_____

Today I am Grateful for:_____

Today I Feel:_____

Today I Learned:_____

Today I treated myself with love and care: Yes   No

ONE DAY AT A TIME: A Self-Care Journal

DATE:_____

Today I promise not to:_____

Today I promise to:_____

Today's Nutrition (circle 1 for each serving you have today):

Veggies:	1	2	3	4	5	6	7	8	9	10	11
Fruit:	1	2	3	4	5	6	7	8	9	10	11
Bread/Starch:	1	2	3	4	5	6	7	8	9	10	11
Dairy:	1	2	3	4	5	6	7	8	9	10	11
Protein:	1	2	3	4	5	6	7	8	9	10	11
Fats, Oils & Sweets	1	2	3	4	5	6	7	8	9	10	
Water:	1	2	3	4	5	6	7	8	9	10	11

Today's Fitness (enter #'s and types that fit your daily routine):

_____ Reps of_____   _____ Reps of_____

_____ Reps of_____   _____ Reps of_____

_____ Reps of_____   _____ Reps of_____

Other:_____

Other:_____

Money I Spent Today:

$_____ for _____ In my budget?   Yes   No

$_____ for _____ In my budget?   Yes   No

$_____ for _____ In my budget?   Yes   No

Something I Cleaned today:_____

Positive Interactions today:_____

_____

What I did towards Spiritual Growth today:_____

Today my biggest Personal Success was:_____

What I did for Someone Else today:_____

Today I am Grateful for:_____

Today I Feel:_____

Today I Learned:_____

Today I treated myself with love and care: Yes   No

ONE DAY AT A TIME: A Self-Care Journal

DATE:_____

Today I promise not to:_____

Today I promise to:_____

Today's Nutrition (circle 1 for each serving you have today):

Veggies:	1	2	3	4	5	6	7	8	9	10	11
Fruit:	1	2	3	4	5	6	7	8	9	10	11
Bread/Starch:	1	2	3	4	5	6	7	8	9	10	11
Dairy:	1	2	3	4	5	6	7	8	9	10	11
Protein:	1	2	3	4	5	6	7	8	9	10	11
Fats, Oils & Sweets	1	2	3	4	5	6	7	8	9	10	
Water:	1	2	3	4	5	6	7	8	9	10	11

Today's Fitness (enter #'s and types that fit your daily routine):

_____ Reps of _____   _____ Reps of_____

_____ Reps of _____   _____ Reps of_____

_____ Reps of _____   _____ Reps of_____

Other:_____

Other:_____

Money I Spent Today:

$_____ for _____ In my budget?   Yes   No

$_____ for _____ In my budget?   Yes   No

$_____ for _____ In my budget?   Yes   No

Something I Cleaned today:_____

Positive Interactions today:_____

_____

What I did towards Spiritual Growth today:_____

Today my biggest Personal Success was:_____

What I did for Someone Else today:_____

Today I am Grateful for:_____

Today I Feel:_____

Today I Learned:_____

Today I treated myself with love and care: Yes   No

ONE DAY AT A TIME: A Self-Care Journal

DATE:_____

Today I promise not to:_____

Today I promise to:_____

Today's Nutrition (circle 1 for each serving you have today):

Veggies:	1	2	3	4	5	6	7	8	9	10	11
Fruit:	1	2	3	4	5	6	7	8	9	10	11
Bread/Starch:	1	2	3	4	5	6	7	8	9	10	11
Dairy:	1	2	3	4	5	6	7	8	9	10	11
Protein:	1	2	3	4	5	6	7	8	9	10	11
Fats, Oils & Sweets	1	2	3	4	5	6	7	8	9	10	
Water:	1	2	3	4	5	6	7	8	9	10	11

Today's Fitness (enter #'s and types that fit your daily routine):

_____ Reps of _____   _____ Reps of_____

_____ Reps of _____   _____ Reps of_____

_____ Reps of _____   _____ Reps of_____

Other:_____

Other:_____

Money I Spent Today:

$_____ for _____ In my budget?   Yes   No

$_____ for _____ In my budget?   Yes   No

$_____ for _____ In my budget?   Yes   No

Something I Cleaned today:_____

Positive Interactions today:_____

_____

What I did towards Spiritual Growth today:_____

Today my biggest Personal Success was:_____

What I did for Someone Else today:_____

Today I am Grateful for:_____

Today I Feel:_____

Today I Learned:_____

Today I treated myself with love and care: Yes   No

ONE DAY AT A TIME: A Self-Care Journal

DATE:_____

Today I promise not to:_____

Today I promise to:_____

Today's Nutrition (circle 1 for each serving you have today):

Veggies:	1	2	3	4	5	6	7	8	9	10	11
Fruit:	1	2	3	4	5	6	7	8	9	10	11
Bread/Starch:	1	2	3	4	5	6	7	8	9	10	11
Dairy:	1	2	3	4	5	6	7	8	9	10	11
Protein:	1	2	3	4	5	6	7	8	9	10	11
Fats, Oils & Sweets	1	2	3	4	5	6	7	8	9	10	
Water:	1	2	3	4	5	6	7	8	9	10	11

Today's Fitness (enter #'s and types that fit your daily routine):

_____ Reps of _____   _____ Reps of_____

_____ Reps of _____   _____ Reps of_____

_____ Reps of _____   _____ Reps of_____

Other:_____

Other:_____

Money I Spent Today:

$_____ for _____ In my budget?   Yes   No

$_____ for _____ In my budget?   Yes   No

$_____ for _____ In my budget?   Yes   No

Something I Cleaned today:_____

Positive Interactions today:_____

_____

What I did towards Spiritual Growth today:_____

Today my biggest Personal Success was:_____

What I did for Someone Else today:_____

Today I am Grateful for:_____

Today I Feel:_____

Today I Learned:_____

Today I treated myself with love and care: Yes   No

ONE DAY AT A TIME: A Self-Care Journal

DATE:_____

Today I promise not to:_____

Today I promise to:_____

Today's Nutrition (circle 1 for each serving you have today):

Veggies:	1	2	3	4	5	6	7	8	9	10	11
Fruit:	1	2	3	4	5	6	7	8	9	10	11
Bread/Starch:	1	2	3	4	5	6	7	8	9	10	11
Dairy:	1	2	3	4	5	6	7	8	9	10	11
Protein:	1	2	3	4	5	6	7	8	9	10	11
Fats, Oils & Sweets	1	2	3	4	5	6	7	8	9	10	
Water:	1	2	3	4	5	6	7	8	9	10	11

Today's Fitness (enter #'s and types that fit your daily routine):

_____ Reps of _____   _____ Reps of_____

_____ Reps of _____   _____ Reps of_____

_____ Reps of _____   _____ Reps of_____

Other:_____

Other:_____

Money I Spent Today:

$_____ for _____ In my budget?   Yes   No

$_____ for _____ In my budget?   Yes   No

$_____ for _____ In my budget?   Yes   No

Something I Cleaned today:_____

Positive Interactions today:_____

_____

What I did towards Spiritual Growth today:_____

Today my biggest Personal Success was:_____

What I did for Someone Else today:_____

Today I am Grateful for:_____

Today I Feel:_____

Today I Learned:_____

Today I treated myself with love and care: Yes   No

ONE DAY AT A TIME: A Self-Care Journal

DATE:_____

Today I promise not to:_____

Today I promise to:_____

Today's Nutrition (circle 1 for each serving you have today):

Veggies:	1	2	3	4	5	6	7	8	9	10	11
Fruit:	1	2	3	4	5	6	7	8	9	10	11
Bread/Starch:	1	2	3	4	5	6	7	8	9	10	11
Dairy:	1	2	3	4	5	6	7	8	9	10	11
Protein:	1	2	3	4	5	6	7	8	9	10	11
Fats, Oils & Sweets	1	2	3	4	5	6	7	8	9	10	
Water:	1	2	3	4	5	6	7	8	9	10	11

Today's Fitness (enter #'s and types that fit your daily routine):

_____ Reps of _____   _____ Reps of _____

_____ Reps of _____   _____ Reps of _____

_____ Reps of _____   _____ Reps of _____

Other:_____

Other:_____

Money I Spent Today:

$_____ for _____ In my budget?   Yes   No

$_____ for _____ In my budget?   Yes   No

$_____ for _____ In my budget?   Yes   No

Something I Cleaned today:_____

Positive Interactions today:_____

_____

What I did towards Spiritual Growth today:_____

Today my biggest Personal Success was:_____

What I did for Someone Else today:_____

Today I am Grateful for:_____

Today I Feel:_____

Today I Learned:_____

Today I treated myself with love and care: Yes   No

ONE DAY AT A TIME: A Self-Care Journal

DATE:_____

Today I promise not to:_____

Today I promise to:_____

Today's Nutrition (circle 1 for each serving you have today):

Veggies:	1	2	3	4	5	6	7	8	9	10	11
Fruit:	1	2	3	4	5	6	7	8	9	10	11
Bread/Starch:	1	2	3	4	5	6	7	8	9	10	11
Dairy:	1	2	3	4	5	6	7	8	9	10	11
Protein:	1	2	3	4	5	6	7	8	9	10	11
Fats, Oils & Sweets	1	2	3	4	5	6	7	8	9	10	
Water:	1	2	3	4	5	6	7	8	9	10	11

Today's Fitness (enter #'s and types that fit your daily routine):

_____ Reps of _____   _____ Reps of_____

_____ Reps of _____   _____ Reps of_____

_____ Reps of _____   _____ Reps of_____

Other:_____

Other:_____

Money I Spent Today:

$_____ for _____ In my budget?   Yes   No

$_____ for _____ In my budget?   Yes   No

$_____ for _____ In my budget?   Yes   No

Something I Cleaned today:_____

Positive Interactions today:_____

_____

What I did towards Spiritual Growth today:_____

Today my biggest Personal Success was:_____

What I did for Someone Else today:_____

Today I am Grateful for:_____

Today I Feel:_____

Today I Learned:_____

Today I treated myself with love and care: Yes   No

ONE DAY AT A TIME: A Self-Care Journal

*DATE:*_____

*Today I promise not to:*_____

*Today I promise to:*_____

Today's Nutrition (circle 1 for each serving you have today):

Veggies:	1	2	3	4	5	6	7	8	9	10	11
Fruit:	1	2	3	4	5	6	7	8	9	10	11
Bread/Starch:	1	2	3	4	5	6	7	8	9	10	11
Dairy:	1	2	3	4	5	6	7	8	9	10	11
Protein:	1	2	3	4	5	6	7	8	9	10	11
Fats, Oils & Sweets	1	2	3	4	5	6	7	8	9	10	
Water:	1	2	3	4	5	6	7	8	9	10	11

Today's Fitness (enter #'s and types that fit your daily routine):

_____ *Reps of* _____   _____ *Reps of*_____

_____ *Reps of* _____   _____ *Reps of*_____

_____ *Reps of* _____   _____ *Reps of*_____

*Other:*_____

*Other:*_____

Money I Spent Today:

$_____ *for* _____ *In my budget?*   Yes   No

$_____ *for* _____ *In my budget?*   Yes   No

$_____ *for* _____ *In my budget?*   Yes   No

*Something I Cleaned today:*_____

*Positive Interactions today:*_____

_____

*What I did towards Spiritual Growth today:*_____

*Today my biggest Personal Success was:*_____

*What I did for Someone Else today:*_____

*Today I am Grateful for:*_____

*Today I Feel:*_____

*Today I Learned:*_____

Today I treated myself with love and care: Yes   No

ONE DAY AT A TIME: A Self-Care Journal

DATE:_____

Today I promise not to:_____

Today I promise to:_____

Today's Nutrition (circle 1 for each serving you have today):

Veggies:	1	2	3	4	5	6	7	8	9	10	11
Fruit:	1	2	3	4	5	6	7	8	9	10	11
Bread/Starch:	1	2	3	4	5	6	7	8	9	10	11
Dairy:	1	2	3	4	5	6	7	8	9	10	11
Protein:	1	2	3	4	5	6	7	8	9	10	11
Fats, Oils & Sweets	1	2	3	4	5	6	7	8	9	10	
Water:	1	2	3	4	5	6	7	8	9	10	11

Today's Fitness (enter #'s and types that fit your daily routine):

_____ Reps of _____   _____ Reps of _____

_____ Reps of _____   _____ Reps of _____

_____ Reps of _____   _____ Reps of _____

Other:_____

Other:_____

Money I Spent Today:

$_____ for _____ In my budget?   Yes   No

$_____ for _____ In my budget?   Yes   No

$_____ for _____ In my budget?   Yes   No

Something I Cleaned today:_____

Positive Interactions today:_____

_____

What I did towards Spiritual Growth today:_____

Today my biggest Personal Success was:_____

What I did for Someone Else today:_____

Today I am Grateful for:_____

Today I Feel:_____

Today I Learned:_____

Today I treated myself with love and care: Yes   No

ONE DAY AT A TIME: A Self-Care Journal

DATE:_____

Today I promise not to:_____

Today I promise to:_____

Today's Nutrition (circle 1 for each serving you have today):

Veggies:	1	2	3	4	5	6	7	8	9	10	11
Fruit:	1	2	3	4	5	6	7	8	9	10	11
Bread/Starch:	1	2	3	4	5	6	7	8	9	10	11
Dairy:	1	2	3	4	5	6	7	8	9	10	11
Protein:	1	2	3	4	5	6	7	8	9	10	11
Fats, Oils & Sweets	1	2	3	4	5	6	7	8	9	10	
Water:	1	2	3	4	5	6	7	8	9	10	11

Today's Fitness (enter #'s and types that fit your daily routine):

_____ Reps of _____   _____ Reps of_____

_____ Reps of _____   _____ Reps of_____

_____ Reps of _____   _____ Reps of_____

Other:_____

Other:_____

Money I Spent Today:

$_____ for _____ In my budget?   Yes   No

$_____ for _____ In my budget?   Yes   No

$_____ for _____ In my budget?   Yes   No

Something I Cleaned today:_____

Positive Interactions today:_____

_____

What I did towards Spiritual Growth today:_____

Today my biggest Personal Success was:_____

What I did for Someone Else today:_____

Today I am Grateful for:_____

Today I Feel:_____

Today I Learned:_____

Today I treated myself with love and care: Yes   No

ONE DAY AT A TIME: A Self-Care Journal

DATE:_____

Today I promise not to:_____

Today I promise to:_____

Today's Nutrition (circle 1 for each serving you have today):

Veggies:	1	2	3	4	5	6	7	8	9	10	11
Fruit:	1	2	3	4	5	6	7	8	9	10	11
Bread/Starch:	1	2	3	4	5	6	7	8	9	10	11
Dairy:	1	2	3	4	5	6	7	8	9	10	11
Protein:	1	2	3	4	5	6	7	8	9	10	11
Fats, Oils & Sweets	1	2	3	4	5	6	7	8	9	10	
Water:	1	2	3	4	5	6	7	8	9	10	11

Today's Fitness (enter #'s and types that fit your daily routine):

_____ Reps of _____   _____ Reps of_____

_____ Reps of _____   _____ Reps of_____

_____ Reps of _____   _____ Reps of_____

Other:_____

Other:_____

Money I Spent Today:

$_____ for _____ In my budget?   Yes   No

$_____ for _____ In my budget?   Yes   No

$_____ for _____ In my budget?   Yes   No

Something I Cleaned today:_____

Positive Interactions today:_____

_____

What I did towards Spiritual Growth today:_____

Today my biggest Personal Success was:_____

What I did for Someone Else today:_____

Today I am Grateful for:_____

Today I Feel:_____

Today I Learned:_____

Today I treated myself with love and care: Yes   No

ONE DAY AT A TIME: A Self-Care Journal

DATE:_____

*Today I promise not to:*_____

*Today I promise to:*_____

Today's Nutrition (circle 1 for each serving you have today):

Veggies:	1	2	3	4	5	6	7	8	9	10	11
Fruit:	1	2	3	4	5	6	7	8	9	10	11
Bread/Starch:	1	2	3	4	5	6	7	8	9	10	11
Dairy:	1	2	3	4	5	6	7	8	9	10	11
Protein:	1	2	3	4	5	6	7	8	9	10	11
Fats, Oils & Sweets	1	2	3	4	5	6	7	8	9	10	
Water:	1	2	3	4	5	6	7	8	9	10	11

Today's Fitness (enter #'s and types that fit your daily routine):

_____ Reps of _____   _____ Reps of_____

_____ Reps of _____   _____ Reps of_____

_____ Reps of _____   _____ Reps of_____

*Other:*_____

*Other:*_____

Money I Spent Today:

$_____ for _____ In my budget?   Yes   No

$_____ for _____ In my budget?   Yes   No

$_____ for _____ In my budget?   Yes   No

*Something I Cleaned today:*_____

*Positive Interactions today:*_____

_____

*What I did towards Spiritual Growth today:*_____

*Today my biggest Personal Success was:*_____

*What I did for Someone Else today:*_____

*Today I am Grateful for:*_____

*Today I Feel:*_____

*Today I Learned:*_____

Today I treated myself with love and care: Yes   No

ONE DAY AT A TIME: A Self-Care Journal

DATE:_____

Today I promise not to:_____

Today I promise to:_____

Today's Nutrition (circle 1 for each serving you have today):

Veggies:	1	2	3	4	5	6	7	8	9	10	11
Fruit:	1	2	3	4	5	6	7	8	9	10	11
Bread/Starch:	1	2	3	4	5	6	7	8	9	10	11
Dairy:	1	2	3	4	5	6	7	8	9	10	11
Protein:	1	2	3	4	5	6	7	8	9	10	11
Fats, Oils & Sweets	1	2	3	4	5	6	7	8	9	10	
Water:	1	2	3	4	5	6	7	8	9	10	11

Today's Fitness (enter #'s and types that fit your daily routine):

_____ Reps of _____   _____ Reps of_____

_____ Reps of _____   _____ Reps of_____

_____ Reps of _____   _____ Reps of_____

Other:_____

Other:_____

Money I Spent Today:

$_____ for _____ In my budget?   Yes   No

$_____ for _____ In my budget?   Yes   No

$_____ for _____ In my budget?   Yes   No

Something I Cleaned today:_____

Positive Interactions today:_____

_____

What I did towards Spiritual Growth today:_____

Today my biggest Personal Success was:_____

What I did for Someone Else today:_____

Today I am Grateful for:_____

Today I Feel:_____

Today I Learned:_____

Today I treated myself with love and care: Yes   No

ONE DAY AT A TIME: A Self-Care Journal

DATE:_____

*Today I promise not to:*_____

*Today I promise to:*_____

Today's Nutrition (circle 1 for each serving you have today):

Veggies:	1	2	3	4	5	6	7	8	9	10	11
Fruit:	1	2	3	4	5	6	7	8	9	10	11
Bread/Starch:	1	2	3	4	5	6	7	8	9	10	11
Dairy:	1	2	3	4	5	6	7	8	9	10	11
Protein:	1	2	3	4	5	6	7	8	9	10	11
Fats, Oils & Sweets	1	2	3	4	5	6	7	8	9	10	
Water:	1	2	3	4	5	6	7	8	9	10	11

Today's Fitness (enter #'s and types that fit your daily routine):

_____ *Reps of* _____   _____ *Reps of*_____

_____ *Reps of* _____   _____ *Reps of*_____

_____ *Reps of* _____   _____ *Reps of*_____

*Other:*_____

*Other:*_____

Money I Spent Today:

$_____ *for* _____ *In my budget?*   *Yes*   *No*

$_____ *for* _____ *In my budget?*   *Yes*   *No*

$_____ *for* _____ *In my budget?*   *Yes*   *No*

*Something I Cleaned today:*_____

*Positive Interactions today:*_____

_____

*What I did towards Spiritual Growth today:*_____

*Today my biggest Personal Success was:*_____

*What I did for Someone Else today:*_____

*Today I am Grateful for:*_____

*Today I Feel:*_____

*Today I Learned:*_____

Today I treated myself with love and care: *Yes*   *No*

ONE DAY AT A TIME: A Self-Care Journal

DATE:_____

Today I promise not to:_____

Today I promise to:_____

Today's Nutrition (circle 1 for each serving you have today):

Veggies:	1	2	3	4	5	6	7	8	9	10	11
Fruit:	1	2	3	4	5	6	7	8	9	10	11
Bread/Starch:	1	2	3	4	5	6	7	8	9	10	11
Dairy:	1	2	3	4	5	6	7	8	9	10	11
Protein:	1	2	3	4	5	6	7	8	9	10	11
Fats, Oils & Sweets	1	2	3	4	5	6	7	8	9	10	
Water:	1	2	3	4	5	6	7	8	9	10	11

Today's Fitness (enter #'s and types that fit your daily routine):

_____ Reps of_____   _____ Reps of_____

_____ Reps of_____   _____ Reps of_____

_____ Reps of_____   _____ Reps of_____

Other:_____

Other:_____

Money I Spent Today:

$_____ for _____ In my budget?   Yes   No

$_____ for _____ In my budget?   Yes   No

$_____ for _____ In my budget?   Yes   No

Something I Cleaned today:_____

Positive Interactions today:_____

_____

What I did towards Spiritual Growth today:_____

Today my biggest Personal Success was:_____

What I did for Someone Else today:_____

Today I am Grateful for:_____

Today I Feel:_____

Today I Learned:_____

Today I treated myself with love and care: Yes   No

ONE DAY AT A TIME: A Self-Care Journal

DATE:_____

Today I promise not to:_____

Today I promise to:_____

Today's Nutrition (circle 1 for each serving you have today):

Veggies:	1	2	3	4	5	6	7	8	9	10	11
Fruit:	1	2	3	4	5	6	7	8	9	10	11
Bread/Starch:	1	2	3	4	5	6	7	8	9	10	11
Dairy:	1	2	3	4	5	6	7	8	9	10	11
Protein:	1	2	3	4	5	6	7	8	9	10	11
Fats, Oils & Sweets	1	2	3	4	5	6	7	8	9	10	
Water:	1	2	3	4	5	6	7	8	9	10	11

Today's Fitness (enter #'s and types that fit your daily routine):

_____ Reps of _____   _____ Reps of_____

_____ Reps of _____   _____ Reps of_____

_____ Reps of _____   _____ Reps of_____

Other:_____

Other:_____

Money I Spent Today:

$_____ for _____ In my budget?   Yes   No

$_____ for _____ In my budget?   Yes   No

$_____ for _____ In my budget?   Yes   No

Something I Cleaned today:_____

Positive Interactions today:_____

_____

What I did towards Spiritual Growth today:_____

Today my biggest Personal Success was:_____

What I did for Someone Else today:_____

Today I am Grateful for:_____

Today I Feel:_____

Today I Learned:_____

Today I treated myself with love and care: Yes   No

ONE DAY AT A TIME: A Self-Care Journal

DATE:_____

Today I promise not to:_____

Today I promise to:_____

Today's Nutrition (circle 1 for each serving you have today):

Veggies:	1	2	3	4	5	6	7	8	9	10	11
Fruit:	1	2	3	4	5	6	7	8	9	10	11
Bread/Starch:	1	2	3	4	5	6	7	8	9	10	11
Dairy:	1	2	3	4	5	6	7	8	9	10	11
Protein:	1	2	3	4	5	6	7	8	9	10	11
Fats, Oils & Sweets	1	2	3	4	5	6	7	8	9	10	
Water:	1	2	3	4	5	6	7	8	9	10	11

Today's Fitness (enter #'s and types that fit your daily routine):

_____ Reps of _____   _____ Reps of_____

_____ Reps of _____   _____ Reps of_____

_____ Reps of _____   _____ Reps of_____

Other:_____

Other:_____

Money I Spent Today:

$_____ for _____ In my budget? Yes No

$_____ for _____ In my budget? Yes No

$_____ for _____ In my budget? Yes No

Something I Cleaned today:_____

Positive Interactions today:_____

_____

What I did towards Spiritual Growth today:_____

Today my biggest Personal Success was:_____

What I did for Someone Else today:_____

Today I am Grateful for:_____

Today I Feel:_____

Today I Learned:_____

Today I treated myself with love and care: Yes   No

ONE DAY AT A TIME: A Self-Care Journal

*DATE:*_____

*Today I promise not to:*_____

*Today I promise to:*_____

Today's Nutrition (circle 1 for each serving you have today):

Veggies:	1	2	3	4	5	6	7	8	9	10	11
Fruit:	1	2	3	4	5	6	7	8	9	10	11
Bread/Starch:	1	2	3	4	5	6	7	8	9	10	11
Dairy:	1	2	3	4	5	6	7	8	9	10	11
Protein:	1	2	3	4	5	6	7	8	9	10	11
Fats, Oils & Sweets	1	2	3	4	5	6	7	8	9	10	
Water:	1	2	3	4	5	6	7	8	9	10	11

Today's Fitness (enter #'s and types that fit your daily routine):

_____ *Reps of*_____   _____ *Reps of*_____

_____ *Reps of*_____   _____ *Reps of*_____

_____ *Reps of*_____   _____ *Reps of*_____

*Other:*_____

*Other:*_____

Money I Spent Today:

$_____ *for* _____ *In my budget?*   *Yes*   *No*

$_____ *for* _____ *In my budget?*   *Yes*   *No*

$_____ *for* _____ *In my budget?*   *Yes*   *No*

*Something I Cleaned today:*_____

*Positive Interactions today:*_____

_____

*What I did towards Spiritual Growth today:*_____

*Today my biggest Personal Success was:*_____

*What I did for Someone Else today:*_____

*Today I am Grateful for:*_____

*Today I Feel:*_____

*Today I Learned:*_____

Today I treated myself with love and care: *Yes*   *No*

ONE DAY AT A TIME: A Self-Care Journal

DATE:_____

Today I promise not to:_____

Today I promise to:_____

Today's Nutrition (circle 1 for each serving you have today):

Veggies:	1	2	3	4	5	6	7	8	9	10	11
Fruit:	1	2	3	4	5	6	7	8	9	10	11
Bread/Starch:	1	2	3	4	5	6	7	8	9	10	11
Dairy:	1	2	3	4	5	6	7	8	9	10	11
Protein:	1	2	3	4	5	6	7	8	9	10	11
Fats, Oils & Sweets	1	2	3	4	5	6	7	8	9	10	
Water:	1	2	3	4	5	6	7	8	9	10	11

Today's Fitness (enter #'s and types that fit your daily routine):

_____ Reps of _____   _____ Reps of_____

_____ Reps of _____   _____ Reps of_____

_____ Reps of _____   _____ Reps of_____

Other:_____

Other:_____

Money I Spent Today:

$_____ for _____ In my budget?   Yes   No

$_____ for _____ In my budget?   Yes   No

$_____ for _____ In my budget?   Yes   No

Something I Cleaned today:_____

Positive Interactions today:_____

_____

What I did towards Spiritual Growth today:_____

Today my biggest Personal Success was:_____

What I did for Someone Else today:_____

Today I am Grateful for:_____

Today I Feel:_____

Today I Learned:_____

Today I treated myself with love and care: Yes   No

ONE DAY AT A TIME: A Self-Care Journal

DATE:_____

Today I promise not to:_____

Today I promise to:_____

Today's Nutrition (circle 1 for each serving you have today):

Veggies:	1	2	3	4	5	6	7	8	9	10	11
Fruit:	1	2	3	4	5	6	7	8	9	10	11
Bread/Starch:	1	2	3	4	5	6	7	8	9	10	11
Dairy:	1	2	3	4	5	6	7	8	9	10	11
Protein:	1	2	3	4	5	6	7	8	9	10	11
Fats, Oils & Sweets	1	2	3	4	5	6	7	8	9	10	
Water:	1	2	3	4	5	6	7	8	9	10	11

Today's Fitness (enter #'s and types that fit your daily routine):

_____ Reps of _____   _____ Reps of_____

_____ Reps of _____   _____ Reps of_____

_____ Reps of _____   _____ Reps of_____

Other:_____

Other:_____

Money I Spent Today:

$_____ for _____ In my budget?   Yes   No

$_____ for _____ In my budget?   Yes   No

$_____ for _____ In my budget?   Yes   No

Something I Cleaned today:_____

Positive Interactions today:_____

_____

What I did towards Spiritual Growth today:_____

Today my biggest Personal Success was:_____

What I did for Someone Else today:_____

Today I am Grateful for:_____

Today I Feel:_____

Today I Learned:_____

Today I treated myself with love and care: Yes   No

ONE DAY AT A TIME: A Self-Care Journal

DATE:_____

Today I promise not to:_____

Today I promise to:_____

Today's Nutrition (circle 1 for each serving you have today):

Veggies:	1	2	3	4	5	6	7	8	9	10	11
Fruit:	1	2	3	4	5	6	7	8	9	10	11
Bread/Starch:	1	2	3	4	5	6	7	8	9	10	11
Dairy:	1	2	3	4	5	6	7	8	9	10	11
Protein:	1	2	3	4	5	6	7	8	9	10	11
Fats, Oils & Sweets	1	2	3	4	5	6	7	8	9	10	
Water:	1	2	3	4	5	6	7	8	9	10	11

Today's Fitness (enter #'s and types that fit your daily routine):

_____ Reps of _____   _____ Reps of_____

_____ Reps of _____   _____ Reps of_____

_____ Reps of _____   _____ Reps of_____

Other:_____

Other:_____

Money I Spent Today:

$_____ for _____ In my budget?   Yes   No

$_____ for _____ In my budget?   Yes   No

$_____ for _____ In my budget?   Yes   No

Something I Cleaned today:_____

Positive Interactions today:_____

_____

What I did towards Spiritual Growth today:_____

Today my biggest Personal Success was:_____

What I did for Someone Else today:_____

Today I am Grateful for:_____

Today I Feel:_____

Today I Learned:_____

Today I treated myself with love and care: Yes   No

ONE DAY AT A TIME: A Self-Care Journal

DATE:_____

Today I promise not to:_____

Today I promise to:_____

Today's Nutrition (circle 1 for each serving you have today):

Veggies:	1	2	3	4	5	6	7	8	9	10	11
Fruit:	1	2	3	4	5	6	7	8	9	10	11
Bread/Starch:	1	2	3	4	5	6	7	8	9	10	11
Dairy:	1	2	3	4	5	6	7	8	9	10	11
Protein:	1	2	3	4	5	6	7	8	9	10	11
Fats, Oils & Sweets	1	2	3	4	5	6	7	8	9	10	
Water:	1	2	3	4	5	6	7	8	9	10	11

Today's Fitness (enter #'s and types that fit your daily routine):

_____ Reps of _____   _____ Reps of_____

_____ Reps of _____   _____ Reps of_____

_____ Reps of _____   _____ Reps of_____

Other:_____

Other:_____

Money I Spent Today:

$_____ for _____ In my budget?   Yes   No

$_____ for _____ In my budget?   Yes   No

$_____ for _____ In my budget?   Yes   No

Something I Cleaned today:_____

Positive Interactions today:_____

_____

What I did towards Spiritual Growth today:_____

Today my biggest Personal Success was:_____

What I did for Someone Else today:_____

Today I am Grateful for:_____

Today I Feel:_____

Today I Learned:_____

Today I treated myself with love and care: Yes   No

ONE DAY AT A TIME: A Self-Care Journal

DATE:_____

Today I promise not to:_____

Today I promise to:_____

Today's Nutrition (circle 1 for each serving you have today):

Veggies:	1	2	3	4	5	6	7	8	9	10	11
Fruit:	1	2	3	4	5	6	7	8	9	10	11
Bread/Starch:	1	2	3	4	5	6	7	8	9	10	11
Dairy:	1	2	3	4	5	6	7	8	9	10	11
Protein:	1	2	3	4	5	6	7	8	9	10	11
Fats, Oils & Sweets	1	2	3	4	5	6	7	8	9	10	
Water:	1	2	3	4	5	6	7	8	9	10	11

Today's Fitness (enter #'s and types that fit your daily routine):

_____ Reps of _____   _____ Reps of_____

_____ Reps of _____   _____ Reps of_____

_____ Reps of _____   _____ Reps of_____

Other:_____

Other:_____

Money I Spent Today:

$_____ for _____ In my budget?   Yes   No

$_____ for _____ In my budget?   Yes   No

$_____ for _____ In my budget?   Yes   No

Something I Cleaned today:_____

Positive Interactions today:_____

_____

What I did towards Spiritual Growth today:_____

Today my biggest Personal Success was:_____

What I did for Someone Else today:_____

Today I am Grateful for:_____

Today I Feel:_____

Today I Learned:_____

Today I treated myself with love and care: Yes   No

ONE DAY AT A TIME: A Self-Care Journal

DATE:_____

Today I promise not to:_____

Today I promise to:_____

Today's Nutrition (circle 1 for each serving you have today):

Veggies:	1	2	3	4	5	6	7	8	9	10	11
Fruit:	1	2	3	4	5	6	7	8	9	10	11
Bread/Starch:	1	2	3	4	5	6	7	8	9	10	11
Dairy:	1	2	3	4	5	6	7	8	9	10	11
Protein:	1	2	3	4	5	6	7	8	9	10	11
Fats, Oils & Sweets	1	2	3	4	5	6	7	8	9	10	
Water:	1	2	3	4	5	6	7	8	9	10	11

Today's Fitness (enter #'s and types that fit your daily routine):

_____ Reps of _____   _____ Reps of_____

_____ Reps of _____   _____ Reps of_____

_____ Reps of _____   _____ Reps of_____

Other:_____

Other:_____

Money I Spent Today:

$_____ for _____ In my budget?   Yes   No

$_____ for _____ In my budget?   Yes   No

$_____ for _____ In my budget?   Yes   No

Something I Cleaned today:_____

Positive Interactions today:_____

_____

What I did towards Spiritual Growth today:_____

Today my biggest Personal Success was:_____

What I did for Someone Else today:_____

Today I am Grateful for:_____

Today I Feel:_____

Today I Learned:_____

Today I treated myself with love and care: Yes   No

ONE DAY AT A TIME: A Self-Care Journal

DATE:_____

Today I promise not to:_____

Today I promise to:_____

Today's Nutrition (circle 1 for each serving you have today):

Veggies:	1	2	3	4	5	6	7	8	9	10	11
Fruit:	1	2	3	4	5	6	7	8	9	10	11
Bread/Starch:	1	2	3	4	5	6	7	8	9	10	11
Dairy:	1	2	3	4	5	6	7	8	9	10	11
Protein:	1	2	3	4	5	6	7	8	9	10	11
Fats, Oils & Sweets	1	2	3	4	5	6	7	8	9	10	
Water:	1	2	3	4	5	6	7	8	9	10	11

Today's Fitness (enter #'s and types that fit your daily routine):

_____ Reps of _____   _____ Reps of_____

_____ Reps of _____   _____ Reps of_____

_____ Reps of _____   _____ Reps of_____

Other:_____

Other:_____

Money I Spent Today:

$_____ for _____ In my budget?   Yes   No

$_____ for _____ In my budget?   Yes   No

$_____ for _____ In my budget?   Yes   No

Something I Cleaned today:_____

Positive Interactions today:_____

_____

What I did towards Spiritual Growth today:_____

Today my biggest Personal Success was:_____

What I did for Someone Else today:_____

Today I am Grateful for:_____

Today I Feel:_____

Today I Learned:_____

Today I treated myself with love and care: Yes   No

ONE DAY AT A TIME: A Self-Care Journal

DATE:_____

Today I promise not to:_____

Today I promise to:_____

Today's Nutrition (circle 1 for each serving you have today):

Veggies:	1	2	3	4	5	6	7	8	9	10	11
Fruit:	1	2	3	4	5	6	7	8	9	10	11
Bread/Starch:	1	2	3	4	5	6	7	8	9	10	11
Dairy:	1	2	3	4	5	6	7	8	9	10	11
Protein:	1	2	3	4	5	6	7	8	9	10	11
Fats, Oils & Sweets	1	2	3	4	5	6	7	8	9	10	
Water:	1	2	3	4	5	6	7	8	9	10	11

Today's Fitness (enter #'s and types that fit your daily routine):

_____ Reps of _____   _____ Reps of_____

_____ Reps of _____   _____ Reps of_____

_____ Reps of _____   _____ Reps of_____

Other:_____

Other:_____

Money I Spent Today:

$_____ for _____ In my budget?   Yes   No

$_____ for _____ In my budget?   Yes   No

$_____ for _____ In my budget?   Yes   No

Something I Cleaned today:_____

Positive Interactions today:_____

_____

What I did towards Spiritual Growth today:_____

Today my biggest Personal Success was:_____

What I did for Someone Else today:_____

Today I am Grateful for:_____

Today I Feel:_____

Today I Learned:_____

Today I treated myself with love and care: Yes   No

ONE DAY AT A TIME: A Self-Care Journal

DATE:_____

Today I promise not to:_____

Today I promise to:_____

Today's Nutrition (circle 1 for each serving you have today):

Veggies:	1	2	3	4	5	6	7	8	9	10	11
Fruit:	1	2	3	4	5	6	7	8	9	10	11
Bread/Starch:	1	2	3	4	5	6	7	8	9	10	11
Dairy:	1	2	3	4	5	6	7	8	9	10	11
Protein:	1	2	3	4	5	6	7	8	9	10	11
Fats, Oils & Sweets	1	2	3	4	5	6	7	8	9	10	
Water:	1	2	3	4	5	6	7	8	9	10	11

Today's Fitness (enter #'s and types that fit your daily routine):

_____ Reps of _____   _____ Reps of_____

_____ Reps of _____   _____ Reps of_____

_____ Reps of _____   _____ Reps of_____

Other:_____

Other:_____

Money I Spent Today:

$_____ for _____ In my budget?   Yes   No

$_____ for _____ In my budget?   Yes   No

$_____ for _____ In my budget?   Yes   No

Something I Cleaned today:_____

Positive Interactions today:_____

_____

What I did towards Spiritual Growth today:_____

Today my biggest Personal Success was:_____

What I did for Someone Else today:_____

Today I am Grateful for:_____

Today I Feel:_____

Today I Learned:_____

Today I treated myself with love and care: Yes   No

ONE DAY AT A TIME: A Self-Care Journal

DATE:_____

Today I promise not to:_____

Today I promise to:_____

Today's Nutrition (circle 1 for each serving you have today):

Veggies:	1	2	3	4	5	6	7	8	9	10	11
Fruit:	1	2	3	4	5	6	7	8	9	10	11
Bread/Starch:	1	2	3	4	5	6	7	8	9	10	11
Dairy:	1	2	3	4	5	6	7	8	9	10	11
Protein:	1	2	3	4	5	6	7	8	9	10	11
Fats, Oils & Sweets	1	2	3	4	5	6	7	8	9	10	
Water:	1	2	3	4	5	6	7	8	9	10	11

Today's Fitness (enter #'s and types that fit your daily routine):

_____ Reps of_____   _____ Reps of_____

_____ Reps of_____   _____ Reps of_____

_____ Reps of_____   _____ Reps of_____

Other:_____

Other:_____

Money I Spent Today:

$_____ for _____ In my budget?   Yes   No

$_____ for _____ In my budget?   Yes   No

$_____ for _____ In my budget?   Yes   No

Something I Cleaned today:_____

Positive Interactions today:_____

_____

What I did towards Spiritual Growth today:_____

Today my biggest Personal Success was:_____

What I did for Someone Else today:_____

Today I am Grateful for:_____

Today I Feel:_____

Today I Learned:_____

Today I treated myself with love and care: Yes   No

ONE DAY AT A TIME: A Self-Care Journal

DATE:_____

Today I promise not to:_____

Today I promise to:_____

Today's Nutrition (circle 1 for each serving you have today):

Veggies:	1	2	3	4	5	6	7	8	9	10	11
Fruit:	1	2	3	4	5	6	7	8	9	10	11
Bread/Starch:	1	2	3	4	5	6	7	8	9	10	11
Dairy:	1	2	3	4	5	6	7	8	9	10	11
Protein:	1	2	3	4	5	6	7	8	9	10	11
Fats, Oils & Sweets	1	2	3	4	5	6	7	8	9	10	
Water:	1	2	3	4	5	6	7	8	9	10	11

Today's Fitness (enter #'s and types that fit your daily routine):

_____ Reps of _____   _____ Reps of_____

_____ Reps of _____   _____ Reps of_____

_____ Reps of _____   _____ Reps of_____

Other:_____

Other:_____

Money I Spent Today:

$_____ for _____ In my budget?   Yes   No

$_____ for _____ In my budget?   Yes   No

$_____ for _____ In my budget?   Yes   No

Something I Cleaned today:_____

Positive Interactions today:_____

_____

What I did towards Spiritual Growth today:_____

Today my biggest Personal Success was:_____

What I did for Someone Else today:_____

Today I am Grateful for:_____

Today I Feel:_____

Today I Learned:_____

Today I treated myself with love and care: Yes   No

ONE DAY AT A TIME: A Self-Care Journal

DATE:_____

Today I promise not to:_____

Today I promise to:_____

Today's Nutrition (circle 1 for each serving you have today):

Veggies:	1	2	3	4	5	6	7	8	9	10	11
Fruit:	1	2	3	4	5	6	7	8	9	10	11
Bread/Starch:	1	2	3	4	5	6	7	8	9	10	11
Dairy:	1	2	3	4	5	6	7	8	9	10	11
Protein:	1	2	3	4	5	6	7	8	9	10	11
Fats, Oils & Sweets	1	2	3	4	5	6	7	8	9	10	
Water:	1	2	3	4	5	6	7	8	9	10	11

Today's Fitness (enter #'s and types that fit your daily routine):

_____ Reps of _____   _____ Reps of_____

_____ Reps of _____   _____ Reps of_____

_____ Reps of _____   _____ Reps of_____

Other:_____

Other:_____

Money I Spent Today:

$_____ for _____ In my budget?   Yes   No

$_____ for _____ In my budget?   Yes   No

$_____ for _____ In my budget?   Yes   No

Something I Cleaned today:_____

Positive Interactions today:_____

_____

What I did towards Spiritual Growth today:_____

Today my biggest Personal Success was:_____

What I did for Someone Else today:_____

Today I am Grateful for:_____

Today I Feel:_____

Today I Learned:_____

Today I treated myself with love and care: Yes   No

ONE DAY AT A TIME: A Self-Care Journal

DATE:_____

Today I promise not to:_____

Today I promise to:_____

Today's Nutrition (circle 1 for each serving you have today):

Veggies:	1	2	3	4	5	6	7	8	9	10	11
Fruit:	1	2	3	4	5	6	7	8	9	10	11
Bread/Starch:	1	2	3	4	5	6	7	8	9	10	11
Dairy:	1	2	3	4	5	6	7	8	9	10	11
Protein:	1	2	3	4	5	6	7	8	9	10	11
Fats, Oils & Sweets	1	2	3	4	5	6	7	8	9	10	
Water:	1	2	3	4	5	6	7	8	9	10	11

Today's Fitness (enter #'s and types that fit your daily routine):

_____ Reps of _____   _____ Reps of_____

_____ Reps of _____   _____ Reps of_____

_____ Reps of _____   _____ Reps of_____

Other:_____

Other:_____

Money I Spent Today:

$_____ for _____ In my budget?   Yes   No

$_____ for _____ In my budget?   Yes   No

$_____ for _____ In my budget?   Yes   No

Something I Cleaned today:_____

Positive Interactions today:_____

_____

What I did towards Spiritual Growth today:_____

Today my biggest Personal Success was:_____

What I did for Someone Else today:_____

Today I am Grateful for:_____

Today I Feel:_____

Today I Learned:_____

Today I treated myself with love and care: Yes   No

ONE DAY AT A TIME: A Self-Care Journal

DATE:_____

Today I promise not to:_____

Today I promise to:_____

Today's Nutrition (circle 1 for each serving you have today):

Veggies:	1	2	3	4	5	6	7	8	9	10	11
Fruit:	1	2	3	4	5	6	7	8	9	10	11
Bread/Starch:	1	2	3	4	5	6	7	8	9	10	11
Dairy:	1	2	3	4	5	6	7	8	9	10	11
Protein:	1	2	3	4	5	6	7	8	9	10	11
Fats, Oils & Sweets	1	2	3	4	5	6	7	8	9	10	
Water:	1	2	3	4	5	6	7	8	9	10	11

Today's Fitness (enter #'s and types that fit your daily routine):

_____ Reps of _____   _____ Reps of_____

_____ Reps of _____   _____ Reps of_____

_____ Reps of _____   _____ Reps of_____

Other:_____

Other:_____

Money I Spent Today:

$_____ for _____ In my budget?   Yes   No

$_____ for _____ In my budget?   Yes   No

$_____ for _____ In my budget?   Yes   No

Something I Cleaned today:_____

Positive Interactions today:_____

_____

What I did towards Spiritual Growth today:_____

Today my biggest Personal Success was:_____

What I did for Someone Else today:_____

Today I am Grateful for:_____

Today I Feel:_____

Today I Learned:_____

Today I treated myself with love and care: Yes   No

ONE DAY AT A TIME: A Self-Care Journal

DATE:_____

Today I promise not to:_____

Today I promise to:_____

Today's Nutrition (circle 1 for each serving you have today):

Veggies:	1	2	3	4	5	6	7	8	9	10	11
Fruit:	1	2	3	4	5	6	7	8	9	10	11
Bread/Starch:	1	2	3	4	5	6	7	8	9	10	11
Dairy:	1	2	3	4	5	6	7	8	9	10	11
Protein:	1	2	3	4	5	6	7	8	9	10	11
Fats, Oils & Sweets	1	2	3	4	5	6	7	8	9	10	
Water:	1	2	3	4	5	6	7	8	9	10	11

Today's Fitness (enter #'s and types that fit your daily routine):

_____ Reps of _____   _____ Reps of_____

_____ Reps of _____   _____ Reps of_____

_____ Reps of _____   _____ Reps of_____

Other:_____

Other:_____

Money I Spent Today:

$_____ for _____ In my budget?   Yes   No

$_____ for _____ In my budget?   Yes   No

$_____ for _____ In my budget?   Yes   No

Something I Cleaned today:_____

Positive Interactions today:_____

_____

What I did towards Spiritual Growth today:_____

Today my biggest Personal Success was:_____

What I did for Someone Else today:_____

Today I am Grateful for:_____

Today I Feel:_____

Today I Learned:_____

Today I treated myself with love and care: Yes   No

ONE DAY AT A TIME: A Self-Care Journal

DATE:_____

Today I promise not to:_____

Today I promise to:_____

Today's Nutrition (circle 1 for each serving you have today):

Veggies:	1	2	3	4	5	6	7	8	9	10	11
Fruit:	1	2	3	4	5	6	7	8	9	10	11
Bread/Starch:	1	2	3	4	5	6	7	8	9	10	11
Dairy:	1	2	3	4	5	6	7	8	9	10	11
Protein:	1	2	3	4	5	6	7	8	9	10	11
Fats, Oils & Sweets	1	2	3	4	5	6	7	8	9	10	
Water:	1	2	3	4	5	6	7	8	9	10	11

Today's Fitness (enter #'s and types that fit your daily routine):

_____ Reps of _____   _____ Reps of_____

_____ Reps of _____   _____ Reps of_____

_____ Reps of _____   _____ Reps of_____

Other:_____

Other:_____

Money I Spent Today:

$_____ for _____ In my budget? Yes No

$_____ for _____ In my budget? Yes No

$_____ for _____ In my budget? Yes No

Something I Cleaned today:_____

Positive Interactions today:_____

_____

What I did towards Spiritual Growth today:_____

Today my biggest Personal Success was:_____

What I did for Someone Else today:_____

Today I am Grateful for:_____

Today I Feel:_____

Today I Learned:_____

Today I treated myself with love and care: Yes   No

ONE DAY AT A TIME: A Self-Care Journal

DATE:_____

Today I promise not to:_____

Today I promise to:_____

Today's Nutrition (circle 1 for each serving you have today):

Veggies:	1	2	3	4	5	6	7	8	9	10	11
Fruit:	1	2	3	4	5	6	7	8	9	10	11
Bread/Starch:	1	2	3	4	5	6	7	8	9	10	11
Dairy:	1	2	3	4	5	6	7	8	9	10	11
Protein:	1	2	3	4	5	6	7	8	9	10	11
Fats, Oils & Sweets	1	2	3	4	5	6	7	8	9	10	
Water:	1	2	3	4	5	6	7	8	9	10	11

Today's Fitness (enter #'s and types that fit your daily routine):

_____ Reps of _____   _____ Reps of_____

_____ Reps of _____   _____ Reps of_____

_____ Reps of _____   _____ Reps of_____

Other:_____

Other:_____

Money I Spent Today:

$_____ for _____ In my budget?   Yes   No

$_____ for _____ In my budget?   Yes   No

$_____ for _____ In my budget?   Yes   No

Something I Cleaned today:_____

Positive Interactions today:_____

_____

What I did towards Spiritual Growth today:_____

Today my biggest Personal Success was:_____

What I did for Someone Else today:_____

Today I am Grateful for:_____

Today I Feel:_____

Today I Learned:_____

Today I treated myself with love and care: Yes   No

ONE DAY AT A TIME: A Self-Care Journal

DATE:_____

Today I promise not to:_____

Today I promise to:_____

Today's Nutrition (circle 1 for each serving you have today):

Veggies:	1	2	3	4	5	6	7	8	9	10	11
Fruit:	1	2	3	4	5	6	7	8	9	10	11
Bread/Starch:	1	2	3	4	5	6	7	8	9	10	11
Dairy:	1	2	3	4	5	6	7	8	9	10	11
Protein:	1	2	3	4	5	6	7	8	9	10	11
Fats, Oils & Sweets	1	2	3	4	5	6	7	8	9	10	
Water:	1	2	3	4	5	6	7	8	9	10	11

Today's Fitness (enter #'s and types that fit your daily routine):

_____ Reps of _____   _____ Reps of_____

_____ Reps of _____   _____ Reps of_____

_____ Reps of _____   _____ Reps of_____

Other:_____

Other:_____

Money I Spent Today:

$_____ for _____ In my budget?   Yes   No

$_____ for _____ In my budget?   Yes   No

$_____ for _____ In my budget?   Yes   No

Something I Cleaned today:_____

Positive Interactions today:_____

_____

What I did towards Spiritual Growth today:_____

Today my biggest Personal Success was:_____

What I did for Someone Else today:_____

Today I am Grateful for:_____

Today I Feel:_____

Today I Learned:_____

Today I treated myself with love and care: Yes   No

ONE DAY AT A TIME: A Self-Care Journal

DATE:_____

Today I promise not to:_____

Today I promise to:_____

Today's Nutrition (circle 1 for each serving you have today):

Veggies:	1	2	3	4	5	6	7	8	9	10	11
Fruit:	1	2	3	4	5	6	7	8	9	10	11
Bread/Starch:	1	2	3	4	5	6	7	8	9	10	11
Dairy:	1	2	3	4	5	6	7	8	9	10	11
Protein:	1	2	3	4	5	6	7	8	9	10	11
Fats, Oils & Sweets	1	2	3	4	5	6	7	8	9	10	
Water:	1	2	3	4	5	6	7	8	9	10	11

Today's Fitness (enter #'s and types that fit your daily routine):

_____ Reps of _____   _____ Reps of_____

_____ Reps of _____   _____ Reps of_____

_____ Reps of _____   _____ Reps of_____

Other:_____

Other:_____

Money I Spent Today:

$_____ for _____ In my budget?   Yes   No

$_____ for _____ In my budget?   Yes   No

$_____ for _____ In my budget?   Yes   No

Something I Cleaned today:_____

Positive Interactions today:_____

_____

What I did towards Spiritual Growth today:_____

Today my biggest Personal Success was:_____

What I did for Someone Else today:_____

Today I am Grateful for:_____

Today I Feel:_____

Today I Learned:_____

Today I treated myself with love and care: Yes   No

ONE DAY AT A TIME: A Self-Care Journal

DATE:_____

Today I promise not to:_____

Today I promise to:_____

Today's Nutrition (circle 1 for each serving you have today):

Veggies:	1	2	3	4	5	6	7	8	9	10	11
Fruit:	1	2	3	4	5	6	7	8	9	10	11
Bread/Starch:	1	2	3	4	5	6	7	8	9	10	11
Dairy:	1	2	3	4	5	6	7	8	9	10	11
Protein:	1	2	3	4	5	6	7	8	9	10	11
Fats, Oils & Sweets	1	2	3	4	5	6	7	8	9	10	
Water:	1	2	3	4	5	6	7	8	9	10	11

Today's Fitness (enter #'s and types that fit your daily routine):

_____ Reps of _____   _____ Reps of_____

_____ Reps of _____   _____ Reps of_____

_____ Reps of _____   _____ Reps of_____

Other:_____

Other:_____

Money I Spent Today:

$_____ for _____ In my budget?   Yes   No

$_____ for _____ In my budget?   Yes   No

$_____ for _____ In my budget?   Yes   No

Something I Cleaned today:_____

Positive Interactions today:_____

_____

What I did towards Spiritual Growth today:_____

Today my biggest Personal Success was:_____

What I did for Someone Else today:_____

Today I am Grateful for:_____

Today I Feel:_____

Today I Learned:_____

Today I treated myself with love and care: Yes   No

ONE DAY AT A TIME: A Self-Care Journal

DATE:_____

Today I promise not to:_____

Today I promise to:_____

Today's Nutrition (circle 1 for each serving you have today):

Veggies:	1	2	3	4	5	6	7	8	9	10	11
Fruit:	1	2	3	4	5	6	7	8	9	10	11
Bread/Starch:	1	2	3	4	5	6	7	8	9	10	11
Dairy:	1	2	3	4	5	6	7	8	9	10	11
Protein:	1	2	3	4	5	6	7	8	9	10	11
Fats, Oils & Sweets	1	2	3	4	5	6	7	8	9	10	
Water:	1	2	3	4	5	6	7	8	9	10	11

Today's Fitness (enter #'s and types that fit your daily routine):

_____ Reps of_____   _____ Reps of_____

_____ Reps of_____   _____ Reps of_____

_____ Reps of_____   _____ Reps of_____

Other:_____

Other:_____

Money I Spent Today:

$_____ for _____ In my budget?   Yes   No

$_____ for _____ In my budget?   Yes   No

$_____ for _____ In my budget?   Yes   No

Something I Cleaned today:_____

Positive Interactions today:_____

_____

What I did towards Spiritual Growth today:_____

Today my biggest Personal Success was:_____

What I did for Someone Else today:_____

Today I am Grateful for:_____

Today I Feel:_____

Today I Learned:_____

Today I treated myself with love and care: Yes   No

ONE DAY AT A TIME: A Self-Care Journal

DATE:_____

Today I promise not to:_____

Today I promise to:_____

Today's Nutrition (circle 1 for each serving you have today):

Veggies:	1	2	3	4	5	6	7	8	9	10	11
Fruit:	1	2	3	4	5	6	7	8	9	10	11
Bread/Starch:	1	2	3	4	5	6	7	8	9	10	11
Dairy:	1	2	3	4	5	6	7	8	9	10	11
Protein:	1	2	3	4	5	6	7	8	9	10	11
Fats, Oils & Sweets	1	2	3	4	5	6	7	8	9	10	
Water:	1	2	3	4	5	6	7	8	9	10	11

Today's Fitness (enter #'s and types that fit your daily routine):

_____ Reps of _____   _____ Reps of_____

_____ Reps of _____   _____ Reps of_____

_____ Reps of _____   _____ Reps of_____

Other:_____

Other:_____

Money I Spent Today:

$_____ for _____ In my budget?   Yes   No

$_____ for _____ In my budget?   Yes   No

$_____ for _____ In my budget?   Yes   No

Something I Cleaned today:_____

Positive Interactions today:_____

_____

What I did towards Spiritual Growth today:_____

Today my biggest Personal Success was:_____

What I did for Someone Else today:_____

Today I am Grateful for:_____

Today I Feel:_____

Today I Learned:_____

Today I treated myself with love and care: Yes   No

ONE DAY AT A TIME: A Self-Care Journal

DATE:_____

Today I promise not to:_____

Today I promise to:_____

Today's Nutrition (circle 1 for each serving you have today):

Veggies:	1	2	3	4	5	6	7	8	9	10	11
Fruit:	1	2	3	4	5	6	7	8	9	10	11
Bread/Starch:	1	2	3	4	5	6	7	8	9	10	11
Dairy:	1	2	3	4	5	6	7	8	9	10	11
Protein:	1	2	3	4	5	6	7	8	9	10	11
Fats, Oils & Sweets	1	2	3	4	5	6	7	8	9	10	
Water:	1	2	3	4	5	6	7	8	9	10	11

Today's Fitness (enter #'s and types that fit your daily routine):

_____ Reps of _____   _____ Reps of_____

_____ Reps of _____   _____ Reps of_____

_____ Reps of _____   _____ Reps of_____

Other:_____

Other:_____

Money I Spent Today:

$_____ for _____ In my budget?   Yes   No

$_____ for _____ In my budget?   Yes   No

$_____ for _____ In my budget?   Yes   No

Something I Cleaned today:_____

Positive Interactions today:_____

_____

What I did towards Spiritual Growth today:_____

Today my biggest Personal Success was:_____

What I did for Someone Else today:_____

Today I am Grateful for:_____

Today I Feel:_____

Today I Learned:_____

Today I treated myself with love and care: Yes   No

ONE DAY AT A TIME: A Self-Care Journal

DATE:_____

Today I promise not to:_____

Today I promise to:_____

Today's Nutrition (circle 1 for each serving you have today):

Veggies:	1	2	3	4	5	6	7	8	9	10	11
Fruit:	1	2	3	4	5	6	7	8	9	10	11
Bread/Starch:	1	2	3	4	5	6	7	8	9	10	11
Dairy:	1	2	3	4	5	6	7	8	9	10	11
Protein:	1	2	3	4	5	6	7	8	9	10	11
Fats, Oils & Sweets	1	2	3	4	5	6	7	8	9	10	
Water:	1	2	3	4	5	6	7	8	9	10	11

Today's Fitness (enter #'s and types that fit your daily routine):

_____ Reps of _____   _____ Reps of_____

_____ Reps of _____   _____ Reps of_____

_____ Reps of _____   _____ Reps of_____

Other:_____

Other:_____

Money I Spent Today:

$_____ for _____ In my budget?   Yes   No

$_____ for _____ In my budget?   Yes   No

$_____ for _____ In my budget?   Yes   No

Something I Cleaned today:_____

Positive Interactions today:_____

_____

What I did towards Spiritual Growth today:_____

Today my biggest Personal Success was:_____

What I did for Someone Else today:_____

Today I am Grateful for:_____

Today I Feel:_____

Today I Learned:_____

Today I treated myself with love and care: Yes   No

ONE DAY AT A TIME: A Self-Care Journal

DATE:_____

Today I promise not to:_____

Today I promise to:_____

Today's Nutrition (circle 1 for each serving you have today):

Veggies:	1	2	3	4	5	6	7	8	9	10	11
Fruit:	1	2	3	4	5	6	7	8	9	10	11
Bread/Starch:	1	2	3	4	5	6	7	8	9	10	11
Dairy:	1	2	3	4	5	6	7	8	9	10	11
Protein:	1	2	3	4	5	6	7	8	9	10	11
Fats, Oils & Sweets	1	2	3	4	5	6	7	8	9	10	
Water:	1	2	3	4	5	6	7	8	9	10	11

Today's Fitness (enter #'s and types that fit your daily routine):

_____ Reps of _____   _____ Reps of_____

_____ Reps of _____   _____ Reps of_____

_____ Reps of _____   _____ Reps of_____

Other:_____

Other:_____

Money I Spent Today:

$_____ for _____ In my budget?   Yes   No

$_____ for _____ In my budget?   Yes   No

$_____ for _____ In my budget?   Yes   No

Something I Cleaned today:_____

Positive Interactions today:_____

_____

What I did towards Spiritual Growth today:_____

Today my biggest Personal Success was:_____

What I did for Someone Else today:_____

Today I am Grateful for:_____

Today I Feel:_____

Today I Learned:_____

Today I treated myself with love and care: Yes   No

ONE DAY AT A TIME: A Self-Care Journal

DATE:_____

Today I promise not to:_____

Today I promise to:_____

Today's Nutrition (circle 1 for each serving you have today):

Veggies:	1	2	3	4	5	6	7	8	9	10	11
Fruit:	1	2	3	4	5	6	7	8	9	10	11
Bread/Starch:	1	2	3	4	5	6	7	8	9	10	11
Dairy:	1	2	3	4	5	6	7	8	9	10	11
Protein:	1	2	3	4	5	6	7	8	9	10	11
Fats, Oils & Sweets	1	2	3	4	5	6	7	8	9	10	
Water:	1	2	3	4	5	6	7	8	9	10	11

Today's Fitness (enter #'s and types that fit your daily routine):

_____ Reps of _____   _____ Reps of_____

_____ Reps of _____   _____ Reps of_____

_____ Reps of _____   _____ Reps of_____

Other:_____

Other:_____

Money I Spent Today:

$_____ for _____ In my budget? Yes No

$_____ for _____ In my budget? Yes No

$_____ for _____ In my budget? Yes No

Something I Cleaned today:_____

Positive Interactions today:_____

_____

What I did towards Spiritual Growth today:_____

Today my biggest Personal Success was:_____

What I did for Someone Else today:_____

Today I am Grateful for:_____

Today I Feel:_____

Today I Learned:_____

Today I treated myself with love and care: Yes   No

ONE DAY AT A TIME: A Self-Care Journal

DATE:_____

Today I promise not to:_____

Today I promise to:_____

Today's Nutrition (circle 1 for each serving you have today):

Veggies:	1	2	3	4	5	6	7	8	9	10	11
Fruit:	1	2	3	4	5	6	7	8	9	10	11
Bread/Starch:	1	2	3	4	5	6	7	8	9	10	11
Dairy:	1	2	3	4	5	6	7	8	9	10	11
Protein:	1	2	3	4	5	6	7	8	9	10	11
Fats, Oils & Sweets	1	2	3	4	5	6	7	8	9	10	
Water:	1	2	3	4	5	6	7	8	9	10	11

Today's Fitness (enter #'s and types that fit your daily routine):

_____ Reps of_____   _____ Reps of_____

_____ Reps of_____   _____ Reps of_____

_____ Reps of_____   _____ Reps of_____

Other:_____

Other:_____

Money I Spent Today:

$_____ for _____ In my budget?   Yes   No

$_____ for _____ In my budget?   Yes   No

$_____ for _____ In my budget?   Yes   No

Something I Cleaned today:_____

Positive Interactions today:_____

_____

What I did towards Spiritual Growth today:_____

Today my biggest Personal Success was:_____

What I did for Someone Else today:_____

Today I am Grateful for:_____

Today I Feel:_____

Today I Learned:_____

Today I treated myself with love and care: Yes   No

ONE DAY AT A TIME: A Self-Care Journal

DATE:_____

Today I promise not to:_____

Today I promise to:_____

Today's Nutrition (circle 1 for each serving you have today):

Veggies:	1	2	3	4	5	6	7	8	9	10	11
Fruit:	1	2	3	4	5	6	7	8	9	10	11
Bread/Starch:	1	2	3	4	5	6	7	8	9	10	11
Dairy:	1	2	3	4	5	6	7	8	9	10	11
Protein:	1	2	3	4	5	6	7	8	9	10	11
Fats, Oils & Sweets	1	2	3	4	5	6	7	8	9	10	
Water:	1	2	3	4	5	6	7	8	9	10	11

Today's Fitness (enter #'s and types that fit your daily routine):

_____ Reps of _____   _____ Reps of_____

_____ Reps of _____   _____ Reps of_____

_____ Reps of _____   _____ Reps of_____

Other:_____

Other:_____

Money I Spent Today:

$_____ for _____ In my budget?   Yes   No

$_____ for _____ In my budget?   Yes   No

$_____ for _____ In my budget?   Yes   No

Something I Cleaned today:_____

Positive Interactions today:_____

_____

What I did towards Spiritual Growth today:_____

Today my biggest Personal Success was:_____

What I did for Someone Else today:_____

Today I am Grateful for:_____

Today I Feel:_____

Today I Learned:_____

Today I treated myself with love and care: Yes   No

ONE DAY AT A TIME: A Self-Care Journal

DATE:_____

Today I promise not to:_____

Today I promise to:_____

Today's Nutrition (circle 1 for each serving you have today):

Veggies:	1	2	3	4	5	6	7	8	9	10	11
Fruit:	1	2	3	4	5	6	7	8	9	10	11
Bread/Starch:	1	2	3	4	5	6	7	8	9	10	11
Dairy:	1	2	3	4	5	6	7	8	9	10	11
Protein:	1	2	3	4	5	6	7	8	9	10	11
Fats, Oils & Sweets	1	2	3	4	5	6	7	8	9	10	
Water:	1	2	3	4	5	6	7	8	9	10	11

Today's Fitness (enter #'s and types that fit your daily routine):

_____ Reps of _____   _____ Reps of_____

_____ Reps of _____   _____ Reps of_____

_____ Reps of _____   _____ Reps of_____

Other:_____

Other:_____

Money I Spent Today:

$_____ for _____ In my budget?   Yes   No

$_____ for _____ In my budget?   Yes   No

$_____ for _____ In my budget?   Yes   No

Something I Cleaned today:_____

Positive Interactions today:_____

_____

What I did towards Spiritual Growth today:_____

Today my biggest Personal Success was:_____

What I did for Someone Else today:_____

Today I am Grateful for:_____

Today I Feel:_____

Today I Learned:_____

Today I treated myself with love and care: Yes   No

ONE DAY AT A TIME: A Self-Care Journal

DATE:_____

Today I promise not to:_____

Today I promise to:_____

Today's Nutrition (circle 1 for each serving you have today):

Veggies:	1	2	3	4	5	6	7	8	9	10	11
Fruit:	1	2	3	4	5	6	7	8	9	10	11
Bread/Starch:	1	2	3	4	5	6	7	8	9	10	11
Dairy:	1	2	3	4	5	6	7	8	9	10	11
Protein:	1	2	3	4	5	6	7	8	9	10	11
Fats, Oils & Sweets	1	2	3	4	5	6	7	8	9	10	
Water:	1	2	3	4	5	6	7	8	9	10	11

Today's Fitness (enter #'s and types that fit your daily routine):

_____ Reps of _____   _____ Reps of_____

_____ Reps of _____   _____ Reps of_____

_____ Reps of _____   _____ Reps of_____

Other:_____

Other:_____

Money I Spent Today:

$_____ for _____ In my budget? Yes No

$_____ for _____ In my budget? Yes No

$_____ for _____ In my budget? Yes No

Something I Cleaned today:_____

Positive Interactions today:_____

_____

What I did towards Spiritual Growth today:_____

Today my biggest Personal Success was:_____

What I did for Someone Else today:_____

Today I am Grateful for:_____

Today I Feel:_____

Today I Learned:_____

Today I treated myself with love and care: Yes   No

ONE DAY AT A TIME: A Self-Care Journal

DATE:_____

Today I promise not to:_____

Today I promise to:_____

Today's Nutrition (circle 1 for each serving you have today):

Veggies:	1	2	3	4	5	6	7	8	9	10	11
Fruit:	1	2	3	4	5	6	7	8	9	10	11
Bread/Starch:	1	2	3	4	5	6	7	8	9	10	11
Dairy:	1	2	3	4	5	6	7	8	9	10	11
Protein:	1	2	3	4	5	6	7	8	9	10	11
Fats, Oils & Sweets	1	2	3	4	5	6	7	8	9	10	
Water:	1	2	3	4	5	6	7	8	9	10	11

Today's Fitness (enter #'s and types that fit your daily routine):

_____ Reps of _____   _____ Reps of_____

_____ Reps of _____   _____ Reps of_____

_____ Reps of _____   _____ Reps of_____

Other:_____

Other:_____

Money I Spent Today:

$_____ for _____ In my budget?   Yes   No

$_____ for _____ In my budget?   Yes   No

$_____ for _____ In my budget?   Yes   No

Something I Cleaned today:_____

Positive Interactions today:_____

_____

What I did towards Spiritual Growth today:_____

Today my biggest Personal Success was:_____

What I did for Someone Else today:_____

Today I am Grateful for:_____

Today I Feel:_____

Today I Learned:_____

Today I treated myself with love and care: Yes   No

ONE DAY AT A TIME: A Self-Care Journal

DATE:_____

Today I promise not to:_____

Today I promise to:_____

Today's Nutrition (circle 1 for each serving you have today):

Veggies:	1	2	3	4	5	6	7	8	9	10	11
Fruit:	1	2	3	4	5	6	7	8	9	10	11
Bread/Starch:	1	2	3	4	5	6	7	8	9	10	11
Dairy:	1	2	3	4	5	6	7	8	9	10	11
Protein:	1	2	3	4	5	6	7	8	9	10	11
Fats, Oils & Sweets	1	2	3	4	5	6	7	8	9	10	
Water:	1	2	3	4	5	6	7	8	9	10	11

Today's Fitness (enter #'s and types that fit your daily routine):

_____ Reps of _____   _____ Reps of_____

_____ Reps of _____   _____ Reps of_____

_____ Reps of _____   _____ Reps of_____

Other:_____

Other:_____

Money I Spent Today:

$_____ for _____ In my budget?   Yes   No

$_____ for _____ In my budget?   Yes   No

$_____ for _____ In my budget?   Yes   No

Something I Cleaned today:_____

Positive Interactions today:_____

_____

What I did towards Spiritual Growth today:_____

Today my biggest Personal Success was:_____

What I did for Someone Else today:_____

Today I am Grateful for:_____

Today I Feel:_____

Today I Learned:_____

Today I treated myself with love and care: Yes   No

ONE DAY AT A TIME: A Self-Care Journal

DATE:_____

Today I promise not to:_____

Today I promise to:_____

Today's Nutrition (circle 1 for each serving you have today):

Veggies:	1	2	3	4	5	6	7	8	9	10	11
Fruit:	1	2	3	4	5	6	7	8	9	10	11
Bread/Starch:	1	2	3	4	5	6	7	8	9	10	11
Dairy:	1	2	3	4	5	6	7	8	9	10	11
Protein:	1	2	3	4	5	6	7	8	9	10	11
Fats, Oils & Sweets	1	2	3	4	5	6	7	8	9	10	
Water:	1	2	3	4	5	6	7	8	9	10	11

Today's Fitness (enter #'s and types that fit your daily routine):

_____ Reps of _____   _____ Reps of_____

_____ Reps of _____   _____ Reps of_____

_____ Reps of _____   _____ Reps of_____

Other:_____

Other:_____

Money I Spent Today:

$_____ for _____ In my budget?   Yes   No

$_____ for _____ In my budget?   Yes   No

$_____ for _____ In my budget?   Yes   No

Something I Cleaned today:_____

Positive Interactions today:_____

_____

What I did towards Spiritual Growth today:_____

Today my biggest Personal Success was:_____

What I did for Someone Else today:_____

Today I am Grateful for:_____

Today I Feel:_____

Today I Learned:_____

Today I treated myself with love and care: Yes   No

ONE DAY AT A TIME: A Self-Care Journal

DATE:_____

Today I promise not to:_____

Today I promise to:_____

Today's Nutrition (circle 1 for each serving you have today):

Veggies:	1	2	3	4	5	6	7	8	9	10	11
Fruit:	1	2	3	4	5	6	7	8	9	10	11
Bread/Starch:	1	2	3	4	5	6	7	8	9	10	11
Dairy:	1	2	3	4	5	6	7	8	9	10	11
Protein:	1	2	3	4	5	6	7	8	9	10	11
Fats, Oils & Sweets	1	2	3	4	5	6	7	8	9	10
Water:	1	2	3	4	5	6	7	8	9	10	11

Today's Fitness (enter #'s and types that fit your daily routine):

_____ Reps of _____   _____ Reps of _____

_____ Reps of _____   _____ Reps of _____

_____ Reps of _____   _____ Reps of _____

Other:_____

Other:_____

Money I Spent Today:

$_____ for _____ In my budget?   Yes   No

$_____ for _____ In my budget?   Yes   No

$_____ for _____ In my budget?   Yes   No

Something I Cleaned today:_____

Positive Interactions today:_____

_____

What I did towards Spiritual Growth today:_____

Today my biggest Personal Success was:_____

What I did for Someone Else today:_____

Today I am Grateful for:_____

Today I Feel:_____

Today I Learned:_____

Today I treated myself with love and care: Yes   No

ONE DAY AT A TIME: A Self-Care Journal

DATE:_____

Today I promise not to:_____

Today I promise to:_____

Today's Nutrition (circle 1 for each serving you have today):

Veggies:	1	2	3	4	5	6	7	8	9	10	11
Fruit:	1	2	3	4	5	6	7	8	9	10	11
Bread/Starch:	1	2	3	4	5	6	7	8	9	10	11
Dairy:	1	2	3	4	5	6	7	8	9	10	11
Protein:	1	2	3	4	5	6	7	8	9	10	11
Fats, Oils & Sweets	1	2	3	4	5	6	7	8	9	10	
Water:	1	2	3	4	5	6	7	8	9	10	11

Today's Fitness (enter #'s and types that fit your daily routine):

_____ Reps of _____   _____ Reps of_____

_____ Reps of _____   _____ Reps of_____

_____ Reps of _____   _____ Reps of_____

Other:_____

Other:_____

Money I Spent Today:

$_____ for _____ In my budget?   Yes   No

$_____ for _____ In my budget?   Yes   No

$_____ for _____ In my budget?   Yes   No

Something I Cleaned today:_____

Positive Interactions today:_____

_____

What I did towards Spiritual Growth today:_____

Today my biggest Personal Success was:_____

What I did for Someone Else today:_____

Today I am Grateful for:_____

Today I Feel:_____

Today I Learned:_____

Today I treated myself with love and care: Yes   No

ONE DAY AT A TIME: A Self-Care Journal

DATE:_____

Today I promise not to:_____

Today I promise to:_____

Today's Nutrition (circle 1 for each serving you have today):

Veggies:	1	2	3	4	5	6	7	8	9	10	11
Fruit:	1	2	3	4	5	6	7	8	9	10	11
Bread/Starch: 1	2	3	4	5	6	7	8	9	10	11
Dairy:	1	2	3	4	5	6	7	8	9	10	11
Protein:	1	2	3	4	5	6	7	8	9	10	11
Fats, Oils & Sweets	1	2	3	4	5	6	7	8	9	10
Water:	1	2	3	4	5	6	7	8	9	10	11

Today's Fitness (enter #'s and types that fit your daily routine):

_____ Reps of _____   _____ Reps of_____

_____ Reps of _____   _____ Reps of_____

_____ Reps of _____   _____ Reps of_____

Other:_____

Other:_____

Money I Spent Today:

$_____ for _____ In my budget?   Yes   No

$_____ for _____ In my budget?   Yes   No

$_____ for _____ In my budget?   Yes   No

Something I Cleaned today:_____

Positive Interactions today:_____

_____

What I did towards Spiritual Growth today:_____

Today my biggest Personal Success was:_____

What I did for Someone Else today:_____

Today I am Grateful for:_____

Today I Feel:_____

Today I Learned:_____

Today I treated myself with love and care: Yes   No

ONE DAY AT A TIME: A Self-Care Journal

DATE:_____

Today I promise not to:_____

Today I promise to:_____

Today's Nutrition (circle 1 for each serving you have today):

Veggies:	1	2	3	4	5	6	7	8	9	10	11
Fruit:	1	2	3	4	5	6	7	8	9	10	11
Bread/Starch:	1	2	3	4	5	6	7	8	9	10	11
Dairy:	1	2	3	4	5	6	7	8	9	10	11
Protein:	1	2	3	4	5	6	7	8	9	10	11
Fats, Oils & Sweets	1	2	3	4	5	6	7	8	9	10	
Water:	1	2	3	4	5	6	7	8	9	10	11

Today's Fitness (enter #'s and types that fit your daily routine):

_____ Reps of_____   _____ Reps of_____

_____ Reps of_____   _____ Reps of_____

_____ Reps of_____   _____ Reps of_____

Other:_____

Other:_____

Money I Spent Today:

$_____ for _____ In my budget?   Yes   No

$_____ for _____ In my budget?   Yes   No

$_____ for _____ In my budget?   Yes   No

Something I Cleaned today:_____

Positive Interactions today:_____

_____

What I did towards Spiritual Growth today:_____

Today my biggest Personal Success was:_____

What I did for Someone Else today:_____

Today I am Grateful for:_____

Today I Feel:_____

Today I Learned:_____

Today I treated myself with love and care: Yes   No

ONE DAY AT A TIME: A Self-Care Journal

DATE:_____

Today I promise not to:_____

Today I promise to:_____

Today's Nutrition (circle 1 for each serving you have today):

Veggies:	1	2	3	4	5	6	7	8	9	10	11
Fruit:	1	2	3	4	5	6	7	8	9	10	11
Bread/Starch:	1	2	3	4	5	6	7	8	9	10	11
Dairy:	1	2	3	4	5	6	7	8	9	10	11
Protein:	1	2	3	4	5	6	7	8	9	10	11
Fats, Oils & Sweets	1	2	3	4	5	6	7	8	9	10	
Water:	1	2	3	4	5	6	7	8	9	10	11

Today's Fitness (enter #'s and types that fit your daily routine):

_____ Reps of _____   _____ Reps of_____

_____ Reps of _____   _____ Reps of_____

_____ Reps of _____   _____ Reps of_____

Other:_____

Other:_____

Money I Spent Today:

$_____ for _____ In my budget?   Yes   No

$_____ for _____ In my budget?   Yes   No

$_____ for _____ In my budget?   Yes   No

Something I Cleaned today:_____

Positive Interactions today:_____

_____

What I did towards Spiritual Growth today:_____

Today my biggest Personal Success was:_____

What I did for Someone Else today:_____

Today I am Grateful for:_____

Today I Feel:_____

Today I Learned:_____

Today I treated myself with love and care: Yes   No

ONE DAY AT A TIME: A Self-Care Journal

DATE:_____

Today I promise not to:_____

Today I promise to:_____

Today's Nutrition (circle 1 for each serving you have today):

Veggies:	1	2	3	4	5	6	7	8	9	10	11
Fruit:	1	2	3	4	5	6	7	8	9	10	11
Bread/Starch:	1	2	3	4	5	6	7	8	9	10	11
Dairy:	1	2	3	4	5	6	7	8	9	10	11
Protein:	1	2	3	4	5	6	7	8	9	10	11
Fats, Oils & Sweets	1	2	3	4	5	6	7	8	9	10	
Water:	1	2	3	4	5	6	7	8	9	10	11

Today's Fitness (enter #'s and types that fit your daily routine):

_____ Reps of _____   _____ Reps of_____

_____ Reps of _____   _____ Reps of_____

_____ Reps of _____   _____ Reps of_____

Other:_____

Other:_____

Money I Spent Today:

$_____ for _____ In my budget?   Yes   No

$_____ for _____ In my budget?   Yes   No

$_____ for _____ In my budget?   Yes   No

Something I Cleaned today:_____

Positive Interactions today:_____

_____

What I did towards Spiritual Growth today:_____

Today my biggest Personal Success was:_____

What I did for Someone Else today:_____

Today I am Grateful for:_____

Today I Feel:_____

Today I Learned:_____

Today I treated myself with love and care: Yes   No

ONE DAY AT A TIME: A Self-Care Journal

DATE:_____

Today I promise not to:_____

Today I promise to:_____

Today's Nutrition (circle 1 for each serving you have today):

Veggies:	1	2	3	4	5	6	7	8	9	10	11
Fruit:	1	2	3	4	5	6	7	8	9	10	11
Bread/Starch:	1	2	3	4	5	6	7	8	9	10	11
Dairy:	1	2	3	4	5	6	7	8	9	10	11
Protein:	1	2	3	4	5	6	7	8	9	10	11
Fats, Oils & Sweets	1	2	3	4	5	6	7	8	9	10	
Water:	1	2	3	4	5	6	7	8	9	10	11

Today's Fitness (enter #'s and types that fit your daily routine):

_____ Reps of _____   _____ Reps of_____

_____ Reps of _____   _____ Reps of_____

_____ Reps of _____   _____ Reps of_____

Other:_____

Other:_____

Money I Spent Today:

$_____ for _____ In my budget?   Yes   No

$_____ for _____ In my budget?   Yes   No

$_____ for _____ In my budget?   Yes   No

Something I Cleaned today:_____

Positive Interactions today:_____

_____

What I did towards Spiritual Growth today:_____

Today my biggest Personal Success was:_____

What I did for Someone Else today:_____

Today I am Grateful for:_____

Today I Feel:_____

Today I Learned:_____

Today I treated myself with love and care: Yes   No

ONE DAY AT A TIME: A Self-Care Journal

DATE:_____

Today I promise not to:_____

Today I promise to:_____

Today's Nutrition (circle 1 for each serving you have today):

Veggies:	1	2	3	4	5	6	7	8	9	10	11
Fruit:	1	2	3	4	5	6	7	8	9	10	11
Bread/Starch:	1	2	3	4	5	6	7	8	9	10	11
Dairy:	1	2	3	4	5	6	7	8	9	10	11
Protein:	1	2	3	4	5	6	7	8	9	10	11
Fats, Oils & Sweets	1	2	3	4	5	6	7	8	9	10	
Water:	1	2	3	4	5	6	7	8	9	10	11

Today's Fitness (enter #'s and types that fit your daily routine):

_____ Reps of _____   _____ Reps of_____

_____ Reps of _____   _____ Reps of_____

_____ Reps of _____   _____ Reps of_____

Other:_____

Other:_____

Money I Spent Today:

$_____ for _____ In my budget?   Yes   No

$_____ for _____ In my budget?   Yes   No

$_____ for _____ In my budget?   Yes   No

Something I Cleaned today:_____

Positive Interactions today:_____

_____

What I did towards Spiritual Growth today:_____

Today my biggest Personal Success was:_____

What I did for Someone Else today:_____

Today I am Grateful for:_____

Today I Feel:_____

Today I Learned:_____

Today I treated myself with love and care: Yes   No

ONE DAY AT A TIME: A Self-Care Journal

*DATE:*_____

*Today I promise not to:*_____

*Today I promise to:*_____

Today's Nutrition (circle 1 for each serving you have today):

Veggies:	*1*	*2*	*3*	*4*	*5*	*6*	*7*	*8*	*9*	*10*	*11*
Fruit:	*1*	*2*	*3*	*4*	*5*	*6*	*7*	*8*	*9*	*10*	*11*
Bread/Starch:	*1*	*2*	*3*	*4*	*5*	*6*	*7*	*8*	*9*	*10*	*11*
Dairy:	*1*	*2*	*3*	*4*	*5*	*6*	*7*	*8*	*9*	*10*	*11*
Protein:	*1*	*2*	*3*	*4*	*5*	*6*	*7*	*8*	*9*	*10*	*11*
Fats, Oils & Sweets	*1*	*2*	*3*	*4*	*5*	*6*	*7*	*8*	*9*	*10*	
Water:	*1*	*2*	*3*	*4*	*5*	*6*	*7*	*8*	*9*	*10*	*11*

Today's Fitness (enter #'s and types that fit your daily routine):

_____ *Reps of* _____   _____ *Reps of*_____

_____ *Reps of* _____   _____ *Reps of*_____

_____ *Reps of* _____   _____ *Reps of*_____

*Other:*_____

*Other:*_____

Money I Spent Today:

$_____ *for* _____ *In my budget?*   *Yes   No*

$_____ *for* _____ *In my budget?*   *Yes   No*

$_____ *for* _____ *In my budget?*   *Yes   No*

*Something I Cleaned today:*_____

*Positive Interactions today:*_____

_____

*What I did towards Spiritual Growth today:*_____

*Today my biggest Personal Success was:*_____

*What I did for Someone Else today:*_____

*Today I am Grateful for:*_____

*Today I Feel:*_____

*Today I Learned:*_____

Today I treated myself with love and care: *Yes   No*

ONE DAY AT A TIME: A Self-Care Journal

DATE:_____

Today I promise not to:_____

Today I promise to:_____

Today's Nutrition (circle 1 for each serving you have today):

Veggies:	1	2	3	4	5	6	7	8	9	10	11
Fruit:	1	2	3	4	5	6	7	8	9	10	11
Bread/Starch:	1	2	3	4	5	6	7	8	9	10	11
Dairy:	1	2	3	4	5	6	7	8	9	10	11
Protein:	1	2	3	4	5	6	7	8	9	10	11
Fats, Oils & Sweets	1	2	3	4	5	6	7	8	9	10	
Water:	1	2	3	4	5	6	7	8	9	10	11

Today's Fitness (enter #'s and types that fit your daily routine):

_____ Reps of _____   _____ Reps of_____

_____ Reps of _____   _____ Reps of_____

_____ Reps of _____   _____ Reps of_____

Other:_____

Other:_____

Money I Spent Today:

$_____ for _____ In my budget?   Yes   No

$_____ for _____ In my budget?   Yes   No

$_____ for _____ In my budget?   Yes   No

Something I Cleaned today:_____

Positive Interactions today:_____

_____

What I did towards Spiritual Growth today:_____

Today my biggest Personal Success was:_____

What I did for Someone Else today:_____

Today I am Grateful for:_____

Today I Feel:_____

Today I Learned:_____

Today I treated myself with love and care: Yes   No

ONE DAY AT A TIME: A Self-Care Journal

DATE:_____

Today I promise not to:_____

Today I promise to:_____

Today's Nutrition (circle 1 for each serving you have today):

Veggies:	1	2	3	4	5	6	7	8	9	10	11
Fruit:	1	2	3	4	5	6	7	8	9	10	11
Bread/Starch:	1	2	3	4	5	6	7	8	9	10	11
Dairy:	1	2	3	4	5	6	7	8	9	10	11
Protein:	1	2	3	4	5	6	7	8	9	10	11
Fats, Oils & Sweets	1	2	3	4	5	6	7	8	9	10	
Water:	1	2	3	4	5	6	7	8	9	10	11

Today's Fitness (enter #'s and types that fit your daily routine):

_____ Reps of_____   _____ Reps of_____

_____ Reps of_____   _____ Reps of_____

_____ Reps of_____   _____ Reps of_____

Other:_____

Other:_____

Money I Spent Today:

$_____ for _____ In my budget?   Yes   No

$_____ for _____ In my budget?   Yes   No

$_____ for _____ In my budget?   Yes   No

Something I Cleaned today:_____

Positive Interactions today:_____

_____

What I did towards Spiritual Growth today:_____

Today my biggest Personal Success was:_____

What I did for Someone Else today:_____

Today I am Grateful for:_____

Today I Feel:_____

Today I Learned:_____

Today I treated myself with love and care: Yes   No

ONE DAY AT A TIME: A Self-Care Journal

DATE:_____

Today I promise not to:_____

Today I promise to:_____

Today's Nutrition (circle 1 for each serving you have today):

Veggies:	1	2	3	4	5	6	7	8	9	10	11
Fruit:	1	2	3	4	5	6	7	8	9	10	11
Bread/Starch:	1	2	3	4	5	6	7	8	9	10	11
Dairy:	1	2	3	4	5	6	7	8	9	10	11
Protein:	1	2	3	4	5	6	7	8	9	10	11
Fats, Oils & Sweets	1	2	3	4	5	6	7	8	9	10	
Water:	1	2	3	4	5	6	7	8	9	10	11

Today's Fitness (enter #'s and types that fit your daily routine):

_____ Reps of _____   _____ Reps of_____

_____ Reps of _____   _____ Reps of_____

_____ Reps of _____   _____ Reps of_____

Other:_____

Other:_____

Money I Spent Today:

$_____ for _____ In my budget?   Yes   No

$_____ for _____ In my budget?   Yes   No

$_____ for _____ In my budget?   Yes   No

Something I Cleaned today:_____

Positive Interactions today:_____

_____

What I did towards Spiritual Growth today:_____

Today my biggest Personal Success was:_____

What I did for Someone Else today:_____

Today I am Grateful for:_____

Today I Feel:_____

Today I Learned:_____

Today I treated myself with love and care: Yes   No

ONE DAY AT A TIME: A Self-Care Journal

*DATE:*_____

*Today I promise not to:*_____

*Today I promise to:*_____

Today's Nutrition (circle 1 for each serving you have today):

Veggies:	1	2	3	4	5	6	7	8	9	10	11
Fruit:	1	2	3	4	5	6	7	8	9	10	11
Bread/Starch:	1	2	3	4	5	6	7	8	9	10	11
Dairy:	1	2	3	4	5	6	7	8	9	10	11
Protein:	1	2	3	4	5	6	7	8	9	10	11
Fats, Oils & Sweets	1	2	3	4	5	6	7	8	9	10	
Water:	1	2	3	4	5	6	7	8	9	10	11

Today's Fitness (enter #'s and types that fit your daily routine):

_____ *Reps of*_____   _____ *Reps of*_____

_____ *Reps of*_____   _____ *Reps of*_____

_____ *Reps of*_____   _____ *Reps of*_____

*Other:*_____

*Other:*_____

Money I Spent Today:

$_____ for _____ In my budget?   *Yes   No*

$_____ for _____ In my budget?   *Yes   No*

$_____ for _____ In my budget?   *Yes   No*

*Something I Cleaned today:*_____

*Positive Interactions today:*_____

_____

*What I did towards Spiritual Growth today:*_____

*Today my biggest Personal Success was:*_____

*What I did for Someone Else today:*_____

*Today I am Grateful for:*_____

*Today I Feel:*_____

*Today I Learned:*_____

Today I treated myself with love and care: *Yes*   *No*

ONE DAY AT A TIME: A Self-Care Journal

DATE:_____

Today I promise not to:_____

Today I promise to:_____

Today's Nutrition (circle 1 for each serving you have today):

Veggies:	1	2	3	4	5	6	7	8	9	10	11
Fruit:	1	2	3	4	5	6	7	8	9	10	11
Bread/Starch:	1	2	3	4	5	6	7	8	9	10	11
Dairy:	1	2	3	4	5	6	7	8	9	10	11
Protein:	1	2	3	4	5	6	7	8	9	10	11
Fats, Oils & Sweets	1	2	3	4	5	6	7	8	9	10	
Water:	1	2	3	4	5	6	7	8	9	10	11

Today's Fitness (enter #'s and types that fit your daily routine):

_____ Reps of _____   _____ Reps of_____

_____ Reps of _____   _____ Reps of_____

_____ Reps of _____   _____ Reps of_____

Other:_____

Other:_____

Money I Spent Today:

$_____ for _____ In my budget?   Yes   No

$_____ for _____ In my budget?   Yes   No

$_____ for _____ In my budget?   Yes   No

Something I Cleaned today:_____

Positive Interactions today:_____

_____

What I did towards Spiritual Growth today:_____

Today my biggest Personal Success was:_____

What I did for Someone Else today:_____

Today I am Grateful for:_____

Today I Feel:_____

Today I Learned:_____

Today I treated myself with love and care: Yes   No

ONE DAY AT A TIME: A Self-Care Journal

DATE:_____

Today I promise not to:_____

Today I promise to:_____

Today's Nutrition (circle 1 for each serving you have today):

Veggies:	1	2	3	4	5	6	7	8	9	10	11
Fruit:	1	2	3	4	5	6	7	8	9	10	11
Bread/Starch:	1	2	3	4	5	6	7	8	9	10	11
Dairy:	1	2	3	4	5	6	7	8	9	10	11
Protein:	1	2	3	4	5	6	7	8	9	10	11
Fats, Oils & Sweets	1	2	3	4	5	6	7	8	9	10	
Water:	1	2	3	4	5	6	7	8	9	10	11

Today's Fitness (enter #'s and types that fit your daily routine):

_____ Reps of _____   _____ Reps of_____

_____ Reps of _____   _____ Reps of_____

_____ Reps of _____   _____ Reps of_____

Other:_____

Other:_____

Money I Spent Today:

$_____ for _____ In my budget?   Yes   No

$_____ for _____ In my budget?   Yes   No

$_____ for _____ In my budget?   Yes   No

Something I Cleaned today:_____

Positive Interactions today:_____

_____

What I did towards Spiritual Growth today:_____

Today my biggest Personal Success was:_____

What I did for Someone Else today:_____

Today I am Grateful for:_____

Today I Feel:_____

Today I Learned:_____

Today I treated myself with love and care: Yes   No

ONE DAY AT A TIME: A Self-Care Journal

DATE:_____

Today I promise not to:_____

Today I promise to:_____

Today's Nutrition (circle 1 for each serving you have today):

Veggies:	1	2	3	4	5	6	7	8	9	10	11
Fruit:	1	2	3	4	5	6	7	8	9	10	11
Bread/Starch:	1	2	3	4	5	6	7	8	9	10	11
Dairy:	1	2	3	4	5	6	7	8	9	10	11
Protein:	1	2	3	4	5	6	7	8	9	10	11
Fats, Oils & Sweets	1	2	3	4	5	6	7	8	9	10	
Water:	1	2	3	4	5	6	7	8	9	10	11

Today's Fitness (enter #'s and types that fit your daily routine):

_____ Reps of _____   _____ Reps of_____

_____ Reps of _____   _____ Reps of_____

_____ Reps of _____   _____ Reps of_____

Other:_____

Other:_____

Money I Spent Today:

$_____ for _____ In my budget?   Yes   No

$_____ for _____ In my budget?   Yes   No

$_____ for _____ In my budget?   Yes   No

Something I Cleaned today:_____

Positive Interactions today:_____

_____

What I did towards Spiritual Growth today:_____

Today my biggest Personal Success was:_____

What I did for Someone Else today:_____

Today I am Grateful for:_____

Today I Feel:_____

Today I Learned:_____

Today I treated myself with love and care: Yes   No

ONE DAY AT A TIME: A Self-Care Journal

*DATE:*_____

*Today I promise not to:*_____

*Today I promise to:*_____

Today's Nutrition (circle 1 for each serving you have today):

Veggies:	*1*	*2*	*3*	*4*	*5*	*6*	*7*	*8*	*9*	*10*	*11*
Fruit:	*1*	*2*	*3*	*4*	*5*	*6*	*7*	*8*	*9*	*10*	*11*
Bread/Starch:	*1*	*2*	*3*	*4*	*5*	*6*	*7*	*8*	*9*	*10*	*11*
Dairy:	*1*	*2*	*3*	*4*	*5*	*6*	*7*	*8*	*9*	*10*	*11*
Protein:	*1*	*2*	*3*	*4*	*5*	*6*	*7*	*8*	*9*	*10*	*11*
Fats, Oils & Sweets	*1*	*2*	*3*	*4*	*5*	*6*	*7*	*8*	*9*	*10*	
Water:	*1*	*2*	*3*	*4*	*5*	*6*	*7*	*8*	*9*	*10*	*11*

Today's Fitness (enter #'s and types that fit your daily routine):

_____ *Reps of*_____   _____ *Reps of*_____

_____ *Reps of*_____   _____ *Reps of*_____

_____ *Reps of*_____   _____ *Reps of*_____

*Other:*_____

*Other:*_____

Money I Spent Today:

$_____ *for* _____ *In my budget?*   *Yes   No*

$_____ *for* _____ *In my budget?*   *Yes   No*

$_____ *for* _____ *In my budget?*   *Yes   No*

*Something I Cleaned today:*_____

*Positive Interactions today:*_____

_____

*What I did towards Spiritual Growth today:*_____

*Today my biggest Personal Success was:*_____

*What I did for Someone Else today:*_____

*Today I am Grateful for:*_____

*Today I Feel:*_____

*Today I Learned:*_____

Today I treated myself with love and care: *Yes*   *No*

ONE DAY AT A TIME: A Self-Care Journal

DATE:_____

Today I promise not to:_____

Today I promise to:_____

Today's Nutrition (circle 1 for each serving you have today):

Veggies:	1	2	3	4	5	6	7	8	9	10	11
Fruit:	1	2	3	4	5	6	7	8	9	10	11
Bread/Starch:	1	2	3	4	5	6	7	8	9	10	11
Dairy:	1	2	3	4	5	6	7	8	9	10	11
Protein:	1	2	3	4	5	6	7	8	9	10	11
Fats, Oils & Sweets	1	2	3	4	5	6	7	8	9	10
Water:	1	2	3	4	5	6	7	8	9	10	11

Today's Fitness (enter #'s and types that fit your daily routine):

_____ Reps of _____   _____ Reps of_____

_____ Reps of _____   _____ Reps of_____

_____ Reps of _____   _____ Reps of_____

Other:_____

Other:_____

Money I Spent Today:

$_____ for _____ In my budget?   Yes   No

$_____ for _____ In my budget?   Yes   No

$_____ for _____ In my budget?   Yes   No

Something I Cleaned today:_____

Positive Interactions today:_____

_____

What I did towards Spiritual Growth today:_____

Today my biggest Personal Success was:_____

What I did for Someone Else today:_____

Today I am Grateful for:_____

Today I Feel:_____

Today I Learned:_____

Today I treated myself with love and care: Yes   No

ONE DAY AT A TIME: A Self-Care Journal

DATE:_____

Today I promise not to:_____

Today I promise to:_____

Today's Nutrition (circle 1 for each serving you have today):

Veggies:	1	2	3	4	5	6	7	8	9	10	11
Fruit:	1	2	3	4	5	6	7	8	9	10	11
Bread/Starch:	1	2	3	4	5	6	7	8	9	10	11
Dairy:	1	2	3	4	5	6	7	8	9	10	11
Protein:	1	2	3	4	5	6	7	8	9	10	11
Fats, Oils & Sweets	1	2	3	4	5	6	7	8	9	10	
Water:	1	2	3	4	5	6	7	8	9	10	11

Today's Fitness (enter #'s and types that fit your daily routine):

_____ Reps of _____   _____ Reps of_____

_____ Reps of _____   _____ Reps of_____

_____ Reps of _____   _____ Reps of_____

Other:_____

Other:_____

Money I Spent Today:

$_____ for _____ In my budget?   Yes   No

$_____ for _____ In my budget?   Yes   No

$_____ for _____ In my budget?   Yes   No

Something I Cleaned today:_____

Positive Interactions today:_____

_____

What I did towards Spiritual Growth today:_____

Today my biggest Personal Success was:_____

What I did for Someone Else today:_____

Today I am Grateful for:_____

Today I Feel:_____

Today I Learned:_____

Today I treated myself with love and care: Yes   No

ONE DAY AT A TIME: A Self-Care Journal

DATE:_____

Today I promise not to:_____

Today I promise to:_____

Today's Nutrition (circle 1 for each serving you have today):

Veggies:	1	2	3	4	5	6	7	8	9	10	11
Fruit:	1	2	3	4	5	6	7	8	9	10	11
Bread/Starch:	1	2	3	4	5	6	7	8	9	10	11
Dairy:	1	2	3	4	5	6	7	8	9	10	11
Protein:	1	2	3	4	5	6	7	8	9	10	11
Fats, Oils & Sweets	1	2	3	4	5	6	7	8	9	10	
Water:	1	2	3	4	5	6	7	8	9	10	11

Today's Fitness (enter #'s and types that fit your daily routine):

_____ Reps of _____   _____ Reps of_____

_____ Reps of _____   _____ Reps of_____

_____ Reps of _____   _____ Reps of_____

Other:_____

Other:_____

Money I Spent Today:

$_____ for _____ In my budget?   Yes   No

$_____ for _____ In my budget?   Yes   No

$_____ for _____ In my budget?   Yes   No

Something I Cleaned today:_____

Positive Interactions today:_____

_____

What I did towards Spiritual Growth today:_____

Today my biggest Personal Success was:_____

What I did for Someone Else today:_____

Today I am Grateful for:_____

Today I Feel:_____

Today I Learned:_____

Today I treated myself with love and care: Yes   No

ONE DAY AT A TIME: A Self-Care Journal

DATE:_____

Today I promise not to:_____

Today I promise to:_____

Today's Nutrition (circle 1 for each serving you have today):

Veggies:	1	2	3	4	5	6	7	8	9	10	11
Fruit:	1	2	3	4	5	6	7	8	9	10	11
Bread/Starch:	1	2	3	4	5	6	7	8	9	10	11
Dairy:	1	2	3	4	5	6	7	8	9	10	11
Protein:	1	2	3	4	5	6	7	8	9	10	11
Fats, Oils & Sweets	1	2	3	4	5	6	7	8	9	10	
Water:	1	2	3	4	5	6	7	8	9	10	11

Today's Fitness (enter #'s and types that fit your daily routine):

_____ Reps of _____   _____ Reps of_____

_____ Reps of _____   _____ Reps of_____

_____ Reps of _____   _____ Reps of_____

Other:_____

Other:_____

Money I Spent Today:

$_____ for _____ In my budget?   Yes   No

$_____ for _____ In my budget?   Yes   No

$_____ for _____ In my budget?   Yes   No

Something I Cleaned today:_____

Positive Interactions today:_____

_____

What I did towards Spiritual Growth today:_____

Today my biggest Personal Success was:_____

What I did for Someone Else today:_____

Today I am Grateful for:_____

Today I Feel:_____

Today I Learned:_____

Today I treated myself with love and care: Yes   No

ONE DAY AT A TIME: A Self-Care Journal

DATE:_____

Today I promise not to:_____

Today I promise to:_____

Today's Nutrition (circle 1 for each serving you have today):

Veggies:	1	2	3	4	5	6	7	8	9	10	11
Fruit:	1	2	3	4	5	6	7	8	9	10	11
Bread/Starch:	1	2	3	4	5	6	7	8	9	10	11
Dairy:	1	2	3	4	5	6	7	8	9	10	11
Protein:	1	2	3	4	5	6	7	8	9	10	11
Fats, Oils & Sweets	1	2	3	4	5	6	7	8	9	10	
Water:	1	2	3	4	5	6	7	8	9	10	11

Today's Fitness (enter #'s and types that fit your daily routine):

_____ Reps of _____   _____ Reps of_____

_____ Reps of _____   _____ Reps of_____

_____ Reps of _____   _____ Reps of_____

Other:_____

Other:_____

Money I Spent Today:

$_____ for _____ In my budget?   Yes   No

$_____ for _____ In my budget?   Yes   No

$_____ for _____ In my budget?   Yes   No

Something I Cleaned today:_____

Positive Interactions today:_____

_____

What I did towards Spiritual Growth today:_____

Today my biggest Personal Success was:_____

What I did for Someone Else today:_____

Today I am Grateful for:_____

Today I Feel:_____

Today I Learned:_____

Today I treated myself with love and care: Yes   No

ONE DAY AT A TIME: A Self-Care Journal

*DATE:*_____

*Today I promise not to:*_____

*Today I promise to:*_____

Today's Nutrition (circle 1 for each serving you have today):

Veggies:	1	2	3	4	5	6	7	8	9	10	11
Fruit:	1	2	3	4	5	6	7	8	9	10	11
Bread/Starch:	1	2	3	4	5	6	7	8	9	10	11
Dairy:	1	2	3	4	5	6	7	8	9	10	11
Protein:	1	2	3	4	5	6	7	8	9	10	11
Fats, Oils & Sweets	1	2	3	4	5	6	7	8	9	10	
Water:	1	2	3	4	5	6	7	8	9	10	11

Today's Fitness (enter #'s and types that fit your daily routine):

_____ *Reps of*_____   _____ *Reps of*_____

_____ *Reps of*_____   _____ *Reps of*_____

_____ *Reps of*_____   _____ *Reps of*_____

*Other:*_____

*Other:*_____

Money I Spent Today:

$_____ *for* _____ *In my budget?*   Yes   No

$_____ *for* _____ *In my budget?*   Yes   No

$_____ *for* _____ *In my budget?*   Yes   No

*Something I Cleaned today:*_____

*Positive Interactions today:*_____

_____

*What I did towards Spiritual Growth today:*_____

*Today my biggest Personal Success was:*_____

*What I did for Someone Else today:*_____

*Today I am Grateful for:*_____

*Today I Feel:*_____

*Today I Learned:*_____

Today I treated myself with love and care: Yes   No

ONE DAY AT A TIME: A Self-Care Journal

DATE:_____

Today I promise not to:_____

Today I promise to:_____

Today's Nutrition (circle 1 for each serving you have today):

Veggies:	1	2	3	4	5	6	7	8	9	10	11
Fruit:	1	2	3	4	5	6	7	8	9	10	11
Bread/Starch:	1	2	3	4	5	6	7	8	9	10	11
Dairy:	1	2	3	4	5	6	7	8	9	10	11
Protein:	1	2	3	4	5	6	7	8	9	10	11
Fats, Oils & Sweets	1	2	3	4	5	6	7	8	9	10	
Water:	1	2	3	4	5	6	7	8	9	10	11

Today's Fitness (enter #'s and types that fit your daily routine):

_____ Reps of _____   _____ Reps of_____

_____ Reps of _____   _____ Reps of_____

_____ Reps of _____   _____ Reps of_____

Other:_____

Other:_____

Money I Spent Today:

$_____ for _____ In my budget?   Yes   No

$_____ for _____ In my budget?   Yes   No

$_____ for _____ In my budget?   Yes   No

Something I Cleaned today:_____

Positive Interactions today:_____

_____

What I did towards Spiritual Growth today:_____

Today my biggest Personal Success was:_____

What I did for Someone Else today:_____

Today I am Grateful for:_____

Today I Feel:_____

Today I Learned:_____

Today I treated myself with love and care: Yes   No

ONE DAY AT A TIME: A Self-Care Journal

DATE:_____

Today I promise not to:_____

Today I promise to:_____

Today's Nutrition (circle 1 for each serving you have today):

Veggies:	1	2	3	4	5	6	7	8	9	10	11
Fruit:	1	2	3	4	5	6	7	8	9	10	11
Bread/Starch:	1	2	3	4	5	6	7	8	9	10	11
Dairy:	1	2	3	4	5	6	7	8	9	10	11
Protein:	1	2	3	4	5	6	7	8	9	10	11
Fats, Oils & Sweets	1	2	3	4	5	6	7	8	9	10	
Water:	1	2	3	4	5	6	7	8	9	10	11

Today's Fitness (enter #'s and types that fit your daily routine):

_____ Reps of _____   _____ Reps of_____

_____ Reps of _____   _____ Reps of_____

_____ Reps of _____   _____ Reps of_____

Other:_____

Other:_____

Money I Spent Today:

$_____ for _____ In my budget?   Yes   No

$_____ for _____ In my budget?   Yes   No

$_____ for _____ In my budget?   Yes   No

Something I Cleaned today:_____

Positive Interactions today:_____

_____

What I did towards Spiritual Growth today:_____

Today my biggest Personal Success was:_____

What I did for Someone Else today:_____

Today I am Grateful for:_____

Today I Feel:_____

Today I Learned:_____

Today I treated myself with love and care: Yes   No

ONE DAY AT A TIME: A Self-Care Journal

DATE:_____

Today I promise not to:_____

Today I promise to:_____

Today's Nutrition (circle 1 for each serving you have today):

Veggies:	1	2	3	4	5	6	7	8	9	10	11
Fruit:	1	2	3	4	5	6	7	8	9	10	11
Bread/Starch:	1	2	3	4	5	6	7	8	9	10	11
Dairy:	1	2	3	4	5	6	7	8	9	10	11
Protein:	1	2	3	4	5	6	7	8	9	10	11
Fats, Oils & Sweets	1	2	3	4	5	6	7	8	9	10	
Water:	1	2	3	4	5	6	7	8	9	10	11

Today's Fitness (enter #'s and types that fit your daily routine):

_____ Reps of _____   _____ Reps of_____

_____ Reps of _____   _____ Reps of_____

_____ Reps of _____   _____ Reps of_____

Other:_____

Other:_____

Money I Spent Today:

$_____ for _____ In my budget?   Yes   No

$_____ for _____ In my budget?   Yes   No

$_____ for _____ In my budget?   Yes   No

Something I Cleaned today:_____

Positive Interactions today:_____

_____

What I did towards Spiritual Growth today:_____

Today my biggest Personal Success was:_____

What I did for Someone Else today:_____

Today I am Grateful for:_____

Today I Feel:_____

Today I Learned:_____

Today I treated myself with love and care: Yes   No

ONE DAY AT A TIME: A Self-Care Journal

DATE:_____

Today I promise not to:_____

Today I promise to:_____

Today's Nutrition (circle 1 for each serving you have today):

Veggies:	1	2	3	4	5	6	7	8	9	10	11
Fruit:	1	2	3	4	5	6	7	8	9	10	11
Bread/Starch:	1	2	3	4	5	6	7	8	9	10	11
Dairy:	1	2	3	4	5	6	7	8	9	10	11
Protein:	1	2	3	4	5	6	7	8	9	10	11
Fats, Oils & Sweets	1	2	3	4	5	6	7	8	9	10	
Water:	1	2	3	4	5	6	7	8	9	10	11

Today's Fitness (enter #'s and types that fit your daily routine):

_____ Reps of_____   _____ Reps of_____

_____ Reps of_____   _____ Reps of_____

_____ Reps of_____   _____ Reps of_____

Other:_____

Other:_____

Money I Spent Today:

$_____ for _____ In my budget?   Yes   No

$_____ for _____ In my budget?   Yes   No

$_____ for _____ In my budget?   Yes   No

Something I Cleaned today:_____

Positive Interactions today:_____

_____

What I did towards Spiritual Growth today:_____

Today my biggest Personal Success was:_____

What I did for Someone Else today:_____

Today I am Grateful for:_____

Today I Feel:_____

Today I Learned:_____

Today I treated myself with love and care: Yes   No

ONE DAY AT A TIME: A Self-Care Journal

DATE:_____

Today I promise not to:_____

Today I promise to:_____

Today's Nutrition (circle 1 for each serving you have today):

Veggies:	1	2	3	4	5	6	7	8	9	10	11
Fruit:	1	2	3	4	5	6	7	8	9	10	11
Bread/Starch:	1	2	3	4	5	6	7	8	9	10	11
Dairy:	1	2	3	4	5	6	7	8	9	10	11
Protein:	1	2	3	4	5	6	7	8	9	10	11
Fats, Oils & Sweets	1	2	3	4	5	6	7	8	9	10	
Water:	1	2	3	4	5	6	7	8	9	10	11

Today's Fitness (enter #'s and types that fit your daily routine):

_____ Reps of _____   _____ Reps of_____

_____ Reps of _____   _____ Reps of_____

_____ Reps of _____   _____ Reps of_____

Other:_____

Other:_____

Money I Spent Today:

$_____ for _____ In my budget?   Yes   No

$_____ for _____ In my budget?   Yes   No

$_____ for _____ In my budget?   Yes   No

Something I Cleaned today:_____

Positive Interactions today:_____

_____

What I did towards Spiritual Growth today:_____

Today my biggest Personal Success was:_____

What I did for Someone Else today:_____

Today I am Grateful for:_____

Today I Feel:_____

Today I Learned:_____

Today I treated myself with love and care: Yes   No

ONE DAY AT A TIME: A Self-Care Journal

*DATE:*_____

*Today I promise not to:*_____

*Today I promise to:*_____

Today's Nutrition (circle 1 for each serving you have today):

Veggies:	1	2	3	4	5	6	7	8	9	10	11
Fruit:	1	2	3	4	5	6	7	8	9	10	11
Bread/Starch:	1	2	3	4	5	6	7	8	9	10	11
Dairy:	1	2	3	4	5	6	7	8	9	10	11
Protein:	1	2	3	4	5	6	7	8	9	10	11
Fats, Oils & Sweets	1	2	3	4	5	6	7	8	9	10	
Water:	1	2	3	4	5	6	7	8	9	10	11

Today's Fitness (enter #'s and types that fit your daily routine):

_____ *Reps of*_____   _____ *Reps of*_____

_____ *Reps of*_____   _____ *Reps of*_____

_____ *Reps of*_____   _____ *Reps of*_____

*Other:*_____

*Other:*_____

Money I Spent Today:

$_____ *for* _____ *In my budget?*   *Yes   No*

$_____ *for* _____ *In my budget?*   *Yes   No*

$_____ *for* _____ *In my budget?*   *Yes   No*

*Something I Cleaned today:*_____

*Positive Interactions today:*_____

_____

*What I did towards Spiritual Growth today:*_____

*Today my biggest Personal Success was:*_____

*What I did for Someone Else today:*_____

*Today I am Grateful for:*_____

*Today I Feel:*_____

*Today I Learned:*_____

Today I treated myself with love and care: *Yes*   *No*

ONE DAY AT A TIME: A Self-Care Journal

DATE:_____

Today I promise not to:_____

Today I promise to:_____

Today's Nutrition (circle 1 for each serving you have today):

Veggies:	1	2	3	4	5	6	7	8	9	10	11
Fruit:	1	2	3	4	5	6	7	8	9	10	11
Bread/Starch: 1	2	3	4	5	6	7	8	9	10	11
Dairy:	1	2	3	4	5	6	7	8	9	10	11
Protein:	1	2	3	4	5	6	7	8	9	10	11
Fats, Oils & Sweets	1	2	3	4	5	6	7	8	9	10
Water:	1	2	3	4	5	6	7	8	9	10	11

Today's Fitness (enter #'s and types that fit your daily routine):

_____ Reps of _____   _____ Reps of_____

_____ Reps of _____   _____ Reps of_____

_____ Reps of _____   _____ Reps of_____

Other:_____

Other:_____

Money I Spent Today:

$_____ for _____ In my budget?   Yes   No

$_____ for _____ In my budget?   Yes   No

$_____ for _____ In my budget?   Yes   No

Something I Cleaned today:_____

Positive Interactions today:_____

_____

What I did towards Spiritual Growth today:_____

Today my biggest Personal Success was:_____

What I did for Someone Else today:_____

Today I am Grateful for:_____

Today I Feel:_____

Today I Learned:_____

Today I treated myself with love and care: Yes   No

ONE DAY AT A TIME: A Self-Care Journal

*DATE:*_____

*Today I promise not to:*_____

*Today I promise to:*_____

Today's Nutrition (circle 1 for each serving you have today):

Veggies:	*1*	*2*	*3*	*4*	*5*	*6*	*7*	*8*	*9*	*10*	*11*
Fruit:	*1*	*2*	*3*	*4*	*5*	*6*	*7*	*8*	*9*	*10*	*11*
Bread/Starch:	*1*	*2*	*3*	*4*	*5*	*6*	*7*	*8*	*9*	*10*	*11*
Dairy:	*1*	*2*	*3*	*4*	*5*	*6*	*7*	*8*	*9*	*10*	*11*
Protein:	*1*	*2*	*3*	*4*	*5*	*6*	*7*	*8*	*9*	*10*	*11*
Fats, Oils & Sweets	*1*	*2*	*3*	*4*	*5*	*6*	*7*	*8*	*9*	*10*	
Water:	*1*	*2*	*3*	*4*	*5*	*6*	*7*	*8*	*9*	*10*	*11*

Today's Fitness (enter #'s and types that fit your daily routine):

_____ *Reps of*_____   _____ *Reps of*_____

_____ *Reps of*_____   _____ *Reps of*_____

_____ *Reps of*_____   _____ *Reps of*_____

*Other:*_____

*Other:*_____

Money I Spent Today:

*$*_____ *for* _____ *In my budget?* *Yes* *No*

*$*_____ *for* _____ *In my budget?* *Yes* *No*

*$*_____ *for* _____ *In my budget?* *Yes* *No*

*Something I Cleaned today:*_____

*Positive Interactions today:*_____

_____

*What I did towards Spiritual Growth today:*_____

*Today my biggest Personal Success was:*_____

*What I did for Someone Else today:*_____

*Today I am Grateful for:*_____

*Today I Feel:*_____

*Today I Learned:*_____

Today I treated myself with love and care: *Yes*   *No*

ONE DAY AT A TIME: A Self-Care Journal

DATE:_____

Today I promise not to:_____

Today I promise to:_____

Today's Nutrition (circle 1 for each serving you have today):

Veggies:	1	2	3	4	5	6	7	8	9	10	11
Fruit:	1	2	3	4	5	6	7	8	9	10	11
Bread/Starch:	1	2	3	4	5	6	7	8	9	10	11
Dairy:	1	2	3	4	5	6	7	8	9	10	11
Protein:	1	2	3	4	5	6	7	8	9	10	11
Fats, Oils & Sweets	1	2	3	4	5	6	7	8	9	10	
Water:	1	2	3	4	5	6	7	8	9	10	11

Today's Fitness (enter #'s and types that fit your daily routine):

_____ Reps of _____   _____ Reps of_____

_____ Reps of _____   _____ Reps of_____

_____ Reps of _____   _____ Reps of_____

Other:_____

Other:_____

Money I Spent Today:

$_____ for _____ In my budget?   Yes   No

$_____ for _____ In my budget?   Yes   No

$_____ for _____ In my budget?   Yes   No

Something I Cleaned today:_____

Positive Interactions today:_____

_____

What I did towards Spiritual Growth today:_____

Today my biggest Personal Success was:_____

What I did for Someone Else today:_____

Today I am Grateful for:_____

Today I Feel:_____

Today I Learned:_____

Today I treated myself with love and care: Yes   No

ONE DAY AT A TIME: A Self-Care Journal

DATE:_____

Today I promise not to:_____

Today I promise to:_____

Today's Nutrition (circle 1 for each serving you have today):

Veggies:	1	2	3	4	5	6	7	8	9	10	11
Fruit:	1	2	3	4	5	6	7	8	9	10	11
Bread/Starch:	1	2	3	4	5	6	7	8	9	10	11
Dairy:	1	2	3	4	5	6	7	8	9	10	11
Protein:	1	2	3	4	5	6	7	8	9	10	11
Fats, Oils & Sweets	1	2	3	4	5	6	7	8	9	10	
Water:	1	2	3	4	5	6	7	8	9	10	11

Today's Fitness (enter #'s and types that fit your daily routine):

_____ Reps of _____   _____ Reps of_____

_____ Reps of _____   _____ Reps of_____

_____ Reps of _____   _____ Reps of_____

Other:_____

Other:_____

Money I Spent Today:

$_____ for _____ In my budget?   Yes   No

$_____ for _____ In my budget?   Yes   No

$_____ for _____ In my budget?   Yes   No

Something I Cleaned today:_____

Positive Interactions today:_____

_____

What I did towards Spiritual Growth today:_____

Today my biggest Personal Success was:_____

What I did for Someone Else today:_____

Today I am Grateful for:_____

Today I Feel:_____

Today I Learned:_____

Today I treated myself with love and care: Yes   No

ONE DAY AT A TIME: A Self-Care Journal

DATE:_____

Today I promise not to:_____

Today I promise to:_____

Today's Nutrition (circle 1 for each serving you have today):

Veggies:	1	2	3	4	5	6	7	8	9	10	11
Fruit:	1	2	3	4	5	6	7	8	9	10	11
Bread/Starch:	1	2	3	4	5	6	7	8	9	10	11
Dairy:	1	2	3	4	5	6	7	8	9	10	11
Protein:	1	2	3	4	5	6	7	8	9	10	11
Fats, Oils & Sweets	1	2	3	4	5	6	7	8	9	10	
Water:	1	2	3	4	5	6	7	8	9	10	11

Today's Fitness (enter #'s and types that fit your daily routine):

_____ Reps of _____   _____ Reps of_____

_____ Reps of _____   _____ Reps of_____

_____ Reps of _____   _____ Reps of_____

Other:_____

Other:_____

Money I Spent Today:

$_____ for _____ In my budget?   Yes   No

$_____ for _____ In my budget?   Yes   No

$_____ for _____ In my budget?   Yes   No

Something I Cleaned today:_____

Positive Interactions today:_____

_____

What I did towards Spiritual Growth today:_____

Today my biggest Personal Success was:_____

What I did for Someone Else today:_____

Today I am Grateful for:_____

Today I Feel:_____

Today I Learned:_____

Today I treated myself with love and care: Yes   No

ONE DAY AT A TIME: A Self-Care Journal

DATE:_____

Today I promise not to:_____

Today I promise to:_____

Today's Nutrition (circle 1 for each serving you have today):

Veggies:	1	2	3	4	5	6	7	8	9	10	11
Fruit:	1	2	3	4	5	6	7	8	9	10	11
Bread/Starch:	1	2	3	4	5	6	7	8	9	10	11
Dairy:	1	2	3	4	5	6	7	8	9	10	11
Protein:	1	2	3	4	5	6	7	8	9	10	11
Fats, Oils & Sweets	1	2	3	4	5	6	7	8	9	10	
Water:	1	2	3	4	5	6	7	8	9	10	11

Today's Fitness (enter #'s and types that fit your daily routine):

_____ Reps of_____   _____ Reps of_____

_____ Reps of_____   _____ Reps of_____

_____ Reps of_____   _____ Reps of_____

Other:_____

Other:_____

Money I Spent Today:

$_____ for _____ In my budget?   Yes   No

$_____ for _____ In my budget?   Yes   No

$_____ for _____ In my budget?   Yes   No

Something I Cleaned today:_____

Positive Interactions today:_____

_____

What I did towards Spiritual Growth today:_____

Today my biggest Personal Success was:_____

What I did for Someone Else today:_____

Today I am Grateful for:_____

Today I Feel:_____

Today I Learned:_____

Today I treated myself with love and care: Yes   No

ONE DAY AT A TIME: A Self-Care Journal

DATE:_____

Today I promise not to:_____

Today I promise to:_____

Today's Nutrition (circle 1 for each serving you have today):

Veggies:	1	2	3	4	5	6	7	8	9	10	11
Fruit:	1	2	3	4	5	6	7	8	9	10	11
Bread/Starch:	1	2	3	4	5	6	7	8	9	10	11
Dairy:	1	2	3	4	5	6	7	8	9	10	11
Protein:	1	2	3	4	5	6	7	8	9	10	11
Fats, Oils & Sweets	1	2	3	4	5	6	7	8	9	10	
Water:	1	2	3	4	5	6	7	8	9	10	11

Today's Fitness (enter #'s and types that fit your daily routine):

_____ Reps of _____   _____ Reps of_____

_____ Reps of _____   _____ Reps of_____

_____ Reps of _____   _____ Reps of_____

Other:_____

Other:_____

Money I Spent Today:

$_____ for _____ In my budget?   Yes   No

$_____ for _____ In my budget?   Yes   No

$_____ for _____ In my budget?   Yes   No

Something I Cleaned today:_____

Positive Interactions today:_____

_____

What I did towards Spiritual Growth today:_____

Today my biggest Personal Success was:_____

What I did for Someone Else today:_____

Today I am Grateful for:_____

Today I Feel:_____

Today I Learned:_____

Today I treated myself with love and care: Yes   No

ONE DAY AT A TIME: A Self-Care Journal

DATE:_____

Today I promise not to:_____

Today I promise to:_____

Today's Nutrition (circle 1 for each serving you have today):

Veggies:	1	2	3	4	5	6	7	8	9	10	11
Fruit:	1	2	3	4	5	6	7	8	9	10	11
Bread/Starch:	1	2	3	4	5	6	7	8	9	10	11
Dairy:	1	2	3	4	5	6	7	8	9	10	11
Protein:	1	2	3	4	5	6	7	8	9	10	11
Fats, Oils & Sweets	1	2	3	4	5	6	7	8	9	10	
Water:	1	2	3	4	5	6	7	8	9	10	11

Today's Fitness (enter #'s and types that fit your daily routine):

_____ Reps of _____   _____ Reps of_____

_____ Reps of _____   _____ Reps of_____

_____ Reps of _____   _____ Reps of_____

Other:_____

Other:_____

Money I Spent Today:

$_____ for _____ In my budget?   Yes   No

$_____ for _____ In my budget?   Yes   No

$_____ for _____ In my budget?   Yes   No

Something I Cleaned today:_____

Positive Interactions today:_____

_____

What I did towards Spiritual Growth today:_____

Today my biggest Personal Success was:_____

What I did for Someone Else today:_____

Today I am Grateful for:_____

Today I Feel:_____

Today I Learned:_____

Today I treated myself with love and care: Yes   No

ONE DAY AT A TIME: A Self-Care Journal

DATE:_____

Today I promise not to:_____

Today I promise to:_____

Today's Nutrition (circle 1 for each serving you have today):

Veggies:	1	2	3	4	5	6	7	8	9	10	11
Fruit:	1	2	3	4	5	6	7	8	9	10	11
Bread/Starch:	1	2	3	4	5	6	7	8	9	10	11
Dairy:	1	2	3	4	5	6	7	8	9	10	11
Protein:	1	2	3	4	5	6	7	8	9	10	11
Fats, Oils & Sweets	1	2	3	4	5	6	7	8	9	10	
Water:	1	2	3	4	5	6	7	8	9	10	11

Today's Fitness (enter #'s and types that fit your daily routine):

_____ Reps of _____   _____ Reps of_____

_____ Reps of _____   _____ Reps of_____

_____ Reps of _____   _____ Reps of_____

Other:_____

Other:_____

Money I Spent Today:

$_____ for _____ In my budget? Yes No

$_____ for _____ In my budget? Yes No

$_____ for _____ In my budget? Yes No

Something I Cleaned today:_____

Positive Interactions today:_____

_____

What I did towards Spiritual Growth today:_____

Today my biggest Personal Success was:_____

What I did for Someone Else today:_____

Today I am Grateful for:_____

Today I Feel:_____

Today I Learned:_____

Today I treated myself with love and care: Yes   No

ONE DAY AT A TIME: A Self-Care Journal

DATE:_____

Today I promise not to:_____

Today I promise to:_____

Today's Nutrition (circle 1 for each serving you have today):

Veggies:	1	2	3	4	5	6	7	8	9	10	11
Fruit:	1	2	3	4	5	6	7	8	9	10	11
Bread/Starch:	1	2	3	4	5	6	7	8	9	10	11
Dairy:	1	2	3	4	5	6	7	8	9	10	11
Protein:	1	2	3	4	5	6	7	8	9	10	11
Fats, Oils & Sweets	1	2	3	4	5	6	7	8	9	10	
Water:	1	2	3	4	5	6	7	8	9	10	11

Today's Fitness (enter #'s and types that fit your daily routine):

_____ Reps of _____   _____ Reps of _____

_____ Reps of _____   _____ Reps of _____

_____ Reps of _____   _____ Reps of _____

Other:_____

Other:_____

Money I Spent Today:

$_____ for _____ In my budget?   Yes   No

$_____ for _____ In my budget?   Yes   No

$_____ for _____ In my budget?   Yes   No

Something I Cleaned today:_____

Positive Interactions today:_____

_____

What I did towards Spiritual Growth today:_____

Today my biggest Personal Success was:_____

What I did for Someone Else today:_____

Today I am Grateful for:_____

Today I Feel:_____

Today I Learned:_____

Today I treated myself with love and care: Yes   No

ONE DAY AT A TIME: A Self-Care Journal

DATE:_____

Today I promise not to:_____

Today I promise to:_____

Today's Nutrition (circle 1 for each serving you have today):

Veggies:	*1*	*2*	*3*	*4*	*5*	*6*	*7*	*8*	*9*	*10*	*11*
Fruit:	*1*	*2*	*3*	*4*	*5*	*6*	*7*	*8*	*9*	*10*	*11*
Bread/Starch:	*1*	*2*	*3*	*4*	*5*	*6*	*7*	*8*	*9*	*10*	*11*
Dairy:	*1*	*2*	*3*	*4*	*5*	*6*	*7*	*8*	*9*	*10*	*11*
Protein:	*1*	*2*	*3*	*4*	*5*	*6*	*7*	*8*	*9*	*10*	*11*
Fats, Oils & Sweets	*1*	*2*	*3*	*4*	*5*	*6*	*7*	*8*	*9*	*10*	
Water:	*1*	*2*	*3*	*4*	*5*	*6*	*7*	*8*	*9*	*10*	*11*

Today's Fitness (enter #'s and types that fit your daily routine):

_____ *Reps of* _____   _____ *Reps of* _____

_____ *Reps of* _____   _____ *Reps of* _____

_____ *Reps of* _____   _____ *Reps of* _____

Other:_____

Other:_____

Money I Spent Today:

$_____ for _____ In my budget?   Yes   No

$_____ for _____ In my budget?   Yes   No

$_____ for _____ In my budget?   Yes   No

Something I Cleaned today:_____

Positive Interactions today:_____

_____

What I did towards Spiritual Growth today:_____

Today my biggest Personal Success was:_____

What I did for Someone Else today:_____

Today I am Grateful for:_____

Today I Feel:_____

Today I Learned:_____

Today I treated myself with love and care: Yes   No

ONE DAY AT A TIME: A Self-Care Journal

DATE:_____

Today I promise not to:_____

Today I promise to:_____

Today's Nutrition (circle 1 for each serving you have today):

Veggies:	1	2	3	4	5	6	7	8	9	10	11
Fruit:	1	2	3	4	5	6	7	8	9	10	11
Bread/Starch:	1	2	3	4	5	6	7	8	9	10	11
Dairy:	1	2	3	4	5	6	7	8	9	10	11
Protein:	1	2	3	4	5	6	7	8	9	10	11
Fats, Oils & Sweets	1	2	3	4	5	6	7	8	9	10	
Water:	1	2	3	4	5	6	7	8	9	10	11

Today's Fitness (enter #'s and types that fit your daily routine):

_____ Reps of _____   _____ Reps of _____

_____ Reps of _____   _____ Reps of _____

_____ Reps of _____   _____ Reps of _____

Other:_____

Other:_____

Money I Spent Today:

$_____ for _____ In my budget?   Yes   No

$_____ for _____ In my budget?   Yes   No

$_____ for _____ In my budget?   Yes   No

Something I Cleaned today:_____

Positive Interactions today:_____

_____

What I did towards Spiritual Growth today:_____

Today my biggest Personal Success was:_____

What I did for Someone Else today:_____

Today I am Grateful for:_____

Today I Feel:_____

Today I Learned:_____

Today I treated myself with love and care: Yes   No

ONE DAY AT A TIME: A Self-Care Journal

DATE:_____

Today I promise not to:_____

Today I promise to:_____

Today's Nutrition (circle 1 for each serving you have today):

Veggies:	1	2	3	4	5	6	7	8	9	10	11
Fruit:	1	2	3	4	5	6	7	8	9	10	11
Bread/Starch:	1	2	3	4	5	6	7	8	9	10	11
Dairy:	1	2	3	4	5	6	7	8	9	10	11
Protein:	1	2	3	4	5	6	7	8	9	10	11
Fats, Oils & Sweets	1	2	3	4	5	6	7	8	9	10	
Water:	1	2	3	4	5	6	7	8	9	10	11

Today's Fitness (enter #'s and types that fit your daily routine):

_____ Reps of _____   _____ Reps of_____

_____ Reps of _____   _____ Reps of_____

_____ Reps of _____   _____ Reps of_____

Other:_____

Other:_____

Money I Spent Today:

$_____ for _____ In my budget?   Yes   No

$_____ for _____ In my budget?   Yes   No

$_____ for _____ In my budget?   Yes   No

Something I Cleaned today:_____

Positive Interactions today:_____

_____

What I did towards Spiritual Growth today:_____

Today my biggest Personal Success was:_____

What I did for Someone Else today:_____

Today I am Grateful for:_____

Today I Feel:_____

Today I Learned:_____

Today I treated myself with love and care: Yes   No

ONE DAY AT A TIME: A Self-Care Journal

DATE:_____

Today I promise not to:_____

Today I promise to:_____

Today's Nutrition (circle 1 for each serving you have today):

Veggies:	1	2	3	4	5	6	7	8	9	10	11
Fruit:	1	2	3	4	5	6	7	8	9	10	11
Bread/Starch:	1	2	3	4	5	6	7	8	9	10	11
Dairy:	1	2	3	4	5	6	7	8	9	10	11
Protein:	1	2	3	4	5	6	7	8	9	10	11
Fats, Oils & Sweets	1	2	3	4	5	6	7	8	9	10	
Water:	1	2	3	4	5	6	7	8	9	10	11

Today's Fitness (enter #'s and types that fit your daily routine):

_____ Reps of _____   _____ Reps of_____

_____ Reps of _____   _____ Reps of_____

_____ Reps of _____   _____ Reps of_____

Other:_____

Other:_____

Money I Spent Today:

$_____ for _____ In my budget?   Yes   No

$_____ for _____ In my budget?   Yes   No

$_____ for _____ In my budget?   Yes   No

Something I Cleaned today:_____

Positive Interactions today:_____

_____

What I did towards Spiritual Growth today:_____

Today my biggest Personal Success was:_____

What I did for Someone Else today:_____

Today I am Grateful for:_____

Today I Feel:_____

Today I Learned:_____

Today I treated myself with love and care: Yes   No

ONE DAY AT A TIME: A Self-Care Journal

DATE:_____

Today I promise not to:_____

Today I promise to:_____

Today's Nutrition (circle 1 for each serving you have today):

Veggies:	1	2	3	4	5	6	7	8	9	10	11
Fruit:	1	2	3	4	5	6	7	8	9	10	11
Bread/Starch:	1	2	3	4	5	6	7	8	9	10	11
Dairy:	1	2	3	4	5	6	7	8	9	10	11
Protein:	1	2	3	4	5	6	7	8	9	10	11
Fats, Oils & Sweets	1	2	3	4	5	6	7	8	9	10
Water:	1	2	3	4	5	6	7	8	9	10	11

Today's Fitness (enter #'s and types that fit your daily routine):

_____ Reps of _____   _____ Reps of_____

_____ Reps of _____   _____ Reps of_____

_____ Reps of _____   _____ Reps of_____

Other:_____

Other:_____

Money I Spent Today:

$_____ for _____ In my budget?   Yes   No

$_____ for _____ In my budget?   Yes   No

$_____ for _____ In my budget?   Yes   No

Something I Cleaned today:_____

Positive Interactions today:_____

_____

What I did towards Spiritual Growth today:_____

Today my biggest Personal Success was:_____

What I did for Someone Else today:_____

Today I am Grateful for:_____

Today I Feel:_____

Today I Learned:_____

Today I treated myself with love and care: Yes   No

ONE DAY AT A TIME: A Self-Care Journal

DATE:_____

Today I promise not to:_____

Today I promise to:_____

Today's Nutrition (circle 1 for each serving you have today):

Veggies:	1	2	3	4	5	6	7	8	9	10	11
Fruit:	1	2	3	4	5	6	7	8	9	10	11
Bread/Starch:	1	2	3	4	5	6	7	8	9	10	11
Dairy:	1	2	3	4	5	6	7	8	9	10	11
Protein:	1	2	3	4	5	6	7	8	9	10	11
Fats, Oils & Sweets	1	2	3	4	5	6	7	8	9	10	
Water:	1	2	3	4	5	6	7	8	9	10	11

Today's Fitness (enter #'s and types that fit your daily routine):

_____ Reps of _____   _____ Reps of_____

_____ Reps of _____   _____ Reps of_____

_____ Reps of _____   _____ Reps of_____

Other:_____

Other:_____

Money I Spent Today:

$_____ for _____ In my budget?   Yes   No

$_____ for _____ In my budget?   Yes   No

$_____ for _____ In my budget?   Yes   No

Something I Cleaned today:_____

Positive Interactions today:_____

_____

What I did towards Spiritual Growth today:_____

Today my biggest Personal Success was:_____

What I did for Someone Else today:_____

Today I am Grateful for:_____

Today I Feel:_____

Today I Learned:_____

Today I treated myself with love and care: Yes   No

ONE DAY AT A TIME: A Self-Care Journal

DATE:_____

Today I promise not to:_____

Today I promise to:_____

Today's Nutrition (circle 1 for each serving you have today):

Veggies:	1	2	3	4	5	6	7	8	9	10	11
Fruit:	1	2	3	4	5	6	7	8	9	10	11
Bread/Starch:	1	2	3	4	5	6	7	8	9	10	11
Dairy:	1	2	3	4	5	6	7	8	9	10	11
Protein:	1	2	3	4	5	6	7	8	9	10	11
Fats, Oils & Sweets	1	2	3	4	5	6	7	8	9	10	
Water:	1	2	3	4	5	6	7	8	9	10	11

Today's Fitness (enter #'s and types that fit your daily routine):

_____ Reps of _____   _____ Reps of_____

_____ Reps of _____   _____ Reps of_____

_____ Reps of _____   _____ Reps of_____

Other:_____

Other:_____

Money I Spent Today:

$_____ for _____ In my budget?   Yes   No

$_____ for _____ In my budget?   Yes   No

$_____ for _____ In my budget?   Yes   No

Something I Cleaned today:_____

Positive Interactions today:_____

_____

What I did towards Spiritual Growth today:_____

Today my biggest Personal Success was:_____

What I did for Someone Else today:_____

Today I am Grateful for:_____

Today I Feel:_____

Today I Learned:_____

Today I treated myself with love and care: Yes   No

ONE DAY AT A TIME: A Self-Care Journal

*DATE:*_____

*Today I promise not to:*_____

*Today I promise to:*_____

Today's Nutrition (circle 1 for each serving you have today):

Veggies:	*1*	*2*	*3*	*4*	*5*	*6*	*7*	*8*	*9*	*10*	*11*
Fruit:	*1*	*2*	*3*	*4*	*5*	*6*	*7*	*8*	*9*	*10*	*11*
Bread/Starch:	*1*	*2*	*3*	*4*	*5*	*6*	*7*	*8*	*9*	*10*	*11*
Dairy:	*1*	*2*	*3*	*4*	*5*	*6*	*7*	*8*	*9*	*10*	*11*
Protein:	*1*	*2*	*3*	*4*	*5*	*6*	*7*	*8*	*9*	*10*	*11*
Fats, Oils & Sweets	*1*	*2*	*3*	*4*	*5*	*6*	*7*	*8*	*9*	*10*	
Water:	*1*	*2*	*3*	*4*	*5*	*6*	*7*	*8*	*9*	*10*	*11*

Today's Fitness (enter #'s and types that fit your daily routine):

_____ *Reps of*_____   _____ *Reps of*_____

_____ *Reps of*_____   _____ *Reps of*_____

_____ *Reps of*_____   _____ *Reps of*_____

*Other:*_____

*Other:*_____

Money I Spent Today:

$_____ *for* _____ *In my budget?*   *Yes*   *No*

$_____ *for* _____ *In my budget?*   *Yes*   *No*

$_____ *for* _____ *In my budget?*   *Yes*   *No*

*Something I Cleaned today:*_____

*Positive Interactions today:*_____

_____

*What I did towards Spiritual Growth today:*_____

*Today my biggest Personal Success was:*_____

*What I did for Someone Else today:*_____

*Today I am Grateful for:*_____

*Today I Feel:*_____

*Today I Learned:*_____

Today I treated myself with love and care: *Yes*   *No*

ONE DAY AT A TIME: A Self-Care Journal

DATE:_____

Today I promise not to:_____

Today I promise to:_____

Today's Nutrition (circle 1 for each serving you have today):

Veggies:	1	2	3	4	5	6	7	8	9	10	11
Fruit:	1	2	3	4	5	6	7	8	9	10	11
Bread/Starch:	1	2	3	4	5	6	7	8	9	10	11
Dairy:	1	2	3	4	5	6	7	8	9	10	11
Protein:	1	2	3	4	5	6	7	8	9	10	11
Fats, Oils & Sweets	1	2	3	4	5	6	7	8	9	10	
Water:	1	2	3	4	5	6	7	8	9	10	11

Today's Fitness (enter #'s and types that fit your daily routine):

_____ Reps of _____   _____ Reps of_____

_____ Reps of _____   _____ Reps of_____

_____ Reps of _____   _____ Reps of_____

Other:_____

Other:_____

Money I Spent Today:

$_____ for _____ In my budget?   Yes   No

$_____ for _____ In my budget?   Yes   No

$_____ for _____ In my budget?   Yes   No

Something I Cleaned today:_____

Positive Interactions today:_____

_____

What I did towards Spiritual Growth today:_____

Today my biggest Personal Success was:_____

What I did for Someone Else today:_____

Today I am Grateful for:_____

Today I Feel:_____

Today I Learned:_____

Today I treated myself with love and care: Yes   No

ONE DAY AT A TIME: A Self-Care Journal

*DATE:*_____

*Today I promise not to:*_____

*Today I promise to:*_____

Today's Nutrition (circle 1 for each serving you have today):

Veggies:	*1*	*2*	*3*	*4*	*5*	*6*	*7*	*8*	*9*	*10*	*11*
Fruit:	*1*	*2*	*3*	*4*	*5*	*6*	*7*	*8*	*9*	*10*	*11*
Bread/Starch:	*1*	*2*	*3*	*4*	*5*	*6*	*7*	*8*	*9*	*10*	*11*
Dairy:	*1*	*2*	*3*	*4*	*5*	*6*	*7*	*8*	*9*	*10*	*11*
Protein:	*1*	*2*	*3*	*4*	*5*	*6*	*7*	*8*	*9*	*10*	*11*
Fats, Oils & Sweets	*1*	*2*	*3*	*4*	*5*	*6*	*7*	*8*	*9*	*10*	
Water:	*1*	*2*	*3*	*4*	*5*	*6*	*7*	*8*	*9*	*10*	*11*

Today's Fitness (enter #'s and types that fit your daily routine):

_____ *Reps of*_____   _____ *Reps of*_____

_____ *Reps of*_____   _____ *Reps of*_____

_____ *Reps of*_____   _____ *Reps of*_____

*Other:*_____

*Other:*_____

Money I Spent Today:

$_____ *for* _____ *In my budget?*   *Yes*   *No*

$_____ *for* _____ *In my budget?*   *Yes*   *No*

$_____ *for* _____ *In my budget?*   *Yes*   *No*

*Something I Cleaned today:*_____

*Positive Interactions today:*_____

_____

*What I did towards Spiritual Growth today:*_____

*Today my biggest Personal Success was:*_____

*What I did for Someone Else today:*_____

*Today I am Grateful for:*_____

*Today I Feel:*_____

*Today I Learned:*_____

Today I treated myself with love and care: *Yes*   *No*

ONE DAY AT A TIME: A Self-Care Journal

DATE:_____

Today I promise not to:_____

Today I promise to:_____

Today's Nutrition (circle 1 for each serving you have today):

Veggies:	1	2	3	4	5	6	7	8	9	10	11
Fruit:	1	2	3	4	5	6	7	8	9	10	11
Bread/Starch:	1	2	3	4	5	6	7	8	9	10	11
Dairy:	1	2	3	4	5	6	7	8	9	10	11
Protein:	1	2	3	4	5	6	7	8	9	10	11
Fats, Oils & Sweets	1	2	3	4	5	6	7	8	9	10	
Water:	1	2	3	4	5	6	7	8	9	10	11

Today's Fitness (enter #'s and types that fit your daily routine):

_____ Reps of _____   _____ Reps of_____

_____ Reps of _____   _____ Reps of_____

_____ Reps of _____   _____ Reps of_____

Other:_____

Other:_____

Money I Spent Today:

$_____ for _____ In my budget?   Yes   No

$_____ for _____ In my budget?   Yes   No

$_____ for _____ In my budget?   Yes   No

Something I Cleaned today:_____

Positive Interactions today:_____

_____

What I did towards Spiritual Growth today:_____

Today my biggest Personal Success was:_____

What I did for Someone Else today:_____

Today I am Grateful for:_____

Today I Feel:_____

Today I Learned:_____

Today I treated myself with love and care: Yes   No

ONE DAY AT A TIME: A Self-Care Journal

*DATE:*_____

*Today I promise not to:*_____

*Today I promise to:*_____

Today's Nutrition (circle 1 for each serving you have today):

Veggies:	*1*	*2*	*3*	*4*	*5*	*6*	*7*	*8*	*9*	*10*	*11*
Fruit:	*1*	*2*	*3*	*4*	*5*	*6*	*7*	*8*	*9*	*10*	*11*
Bread/Starch:	*1*	*2*	*3*	*4*	*5*	*6*	*7*	*8*	*9*	*10*	*11*
Dairy:	*1*	*2*	*3*	*4*	*5*	*6*	*7*	*8*	*9*	*10*	*11*
Protein:	*1*	*2*	*3*	*4*	*5*	*6*	*7*	*8*	*9*	*10*	*11*
Fats, Oils & Sweets	*1*	*2*	*3*	*4*	*5*	*6*	*7*	*8*	*9*	*10*	
Water:	*1*	*2*	*3*	*4*	*5*	*6*	*7*	*8*	*9*	*10*	*11*

Today's Fitness (enter #'s and types that fit your daily routine):

_____ *Reps of* _____   _____ *Reps of*_____

_____ *Reps of* _____   _____ *Reps of*_____

_____ *Reps of* _____   _____ *Reps of*_____

*Other:*_____

*Other:*_____

Money I Spent Today:

$_____ *for* _____ *In my budget?*   *Yes*   *No*

$_____ *for* _____ *In my budget?*   *Yes*   *No*

$_____ *for* _____ *In my budget?*   *Yes*   *No*

*Something I Cleaned today:*_____

*Positive Interactions today:*_____

_____

*What I did towards Spiritual Growth today:*_____

*Today my biggest Personal Success was:*_____

*What I did for Someone Else today:*_____

*Today I am Grateful for:*_____

*Today I Feel:*_____

*Today I Learned:*_____

Today I treated myself with love and care: *Yes*   *No*

ONE DAY AT A TIME: A Self-Care Journal

DATE:_____

Today I promise not to:_____

Today I promise to:_____

Today's Nutrition (circle 1 for each serving you have today):

Veggies:	1	2	3	4	5	6	7	8	9	10	11
Fruit:	1	2	3	4	5	6	7	8	9	10	11
Bread/Starch:	1	2	3	4	5	6	7	8	9	10	11
Dairy:	1	2	3	4	5	6	7	8	9	10	11
Protein:	1	2	3	4	5	6	7	8	9	10	11
Fats, Oils & Sweets	1	2	3	4	5	6	7	8	9	10	
Water:	1	2	3	4	5	6	7	8	9	10	11

Today's Fitness (enter #'s and types that fit your daily routine):

_____ Reps of _____   _____ Reps of_____

_____ Reps of _____   _____ Reps of_____

_____ Reps of _____   _____ Reps of_____

Other:_____

Other:_____

Money I Spent Today:

$_____ for _____ In my budget?   Yes   No

$_____ for _____ In my budget?   Yes   No

$_____ for _____ In my budget?   Yes   No

Something I Cleaned today:_____

Positive Interactions today:_____

_____

What I did towards Spiritual Growth today:_____

Today my biggest Personal Success was:_____

What I did for Someone Else today:_____

Today I am Grateful for:_____

Today I Feel:_____

Today I Learned:_____

Today I treated myself with love and care: Yes   No

ONE DAY AT A TIME: A Self-Care Journal

DATE:_____

Today I promise not to:_____

Today I promise to:_____

Today's Nutrition (circle 1 for each serving you have today):

Veggies:	1	2	3	4	5	6	7	8	9	10	11
Fruit:	1	2	3	4	5	6	7	8	9	10	11
Bread/Starch:	1	2	3	4	5	6	7	8	9	10	11
Dairy:	1	2	3	4	5	6	7	8	9	10	11
Protein:	1	2	3	4	5	6	7	8	9	10	11
Fats, Oils & Sweets	1	2	3	4	5	6	7	8	9	10	
Water:	1	2	3	4	5	6	7	8	9	10	11

Today's Fitness (enter #'s and types that fit your daily routine):

_____ Reps of_____   _____ Reps of_____

_____ Reps of_____   _____ Reps of_____

_____ Reps of_____   _____ Reps of_____

Other:_____

Other:_____

Money I Spent Today:

$_____ for _____ In my budget?   Yes   No

$_____ for _____ In my budget?   Yes   No

$_____ for _____ In my budget?   Yes   No

Something I Cleaned today:_____

Positive Interactions today:_____

_____

What I did towards Spiritual Growth today:_____

Today my biggest Personal Success was:_____

What I did for Someone Else today:_____

Today I am Grateful for:_____

Today I Feel:_____

Today I Learned:_____

Today I treated myself with love and care: Yes   No

ONE DAY AT A TIME: A Self-Care Journal

DATE:_____

Today I promise not to:_____

Today I promise to:_____

Today's Nutrition (circle 1 for each serving you have today):

Veggies:	1	2	3	4	5	6	7	8	9	10	11
Fruit:	1	2	3	4	5	6	7	8	9	10	11
Bread/Starch:	1	2	3	4	5	6	7	8	9	10	11
Dairy:	1	2	3	4	5	6	7	8	9	10	11
Protein:	1	2	3	4	5	6	7	8	9	10	11
Fats, Oils & Sweets	1	2	3	4	5	6	7	8	9	10	
Water:	1	2	3	4	5	6	7	8	9	10	11

Today's Fitness (enter #'s and types that fit your daily routine):

_____ Reps of _____   _____ Reps of_____

_____ Reps of _____   _____ Reps of_____

_____ Reps of _____   _____ Reps of_____

Other:_____

Other:_____

Money I Spent Today:

$_____ for _____ In my budget?   Yes   No

$_____ for _____ In my budget?   Yes   No

$_____ for _____ In my budget?   Yes   No

Something I Cleaned today:_____

Positive Interactions today:_____

_____

What I did towards Spiritual Growth today:_____

Today my biggest Personal Success was:_____

What I did for Someone Else today:_____

Today I am Grateful for:_____

Today I Feel:_____

Today I Learned:_____

Today I treated myself with love and care: Yes   No

ONE DAY AT A TIME: A Self-Care Journal

DATE:_____

Today I promise not to:_____

Today I promise to:_____

Today's Nutrition (circle 1 for each serving you have today):

Veggies:	1	2	3	4	5	6	7	8	9	10	11
Fruit:	1	2	3	4	5	6	7	8	9	10	11
Bread/Starch:	1	2	3	4	5	6	7	8	9	10	11
Dairy:	1	2	3	4	5	6	7	8	9	10	11
Protein:	1	2	3	4	5	6	7	8	9	10	11
Fats, Oils & Sweets	1	2	3	4	5	6	7	8	9	10	
Water:	1	2	3	4	5	6	7	8	9	10	11

Today's Fitness (enter #'s and types that fit your daily routine):

_____ Reps of _____   _____ Reps of_____

_____ Reps of _____   _____ Reps of_____

_____ Reps of _____   _____ Reps of_____

Other:_____

Other:_____

Money I Spent Today:

$_____ for _____ In my budget?   Yes   No

$_____ for _____ In my budget?   Yes   No

$_____ for _____ In my budget?   Yes   No

Something I Cleaned today:_____

Positive Interactions today:_____

_____

What I did towards Spiritual Growth today:_____

Today my biggest Personal Success was:_____

What I did for Someone Else today:_____

Today I am Grateful for:_____

Today I Feel:_____

Today I Learned:_____

Today I treated myself with love and care: Yes   No

ONE DAY AT A TIME: A Self-Care Journal

DATE:_____

Today I promise not to:_____

Today I promise to:_____

Today's Nutrition (circle 1 for each serving you have today):

Veggies:	1	2	3	4	5	6	7	8	9	10	11
Fruit:	1	2	3	4	5	6	7	8	9	10	11
Bread/Starch:	1	2	3	4	5	6	7	8	9	10	11
Dairy:	1	2	3	4	5	6	7	8	9	10	11
Protein:	1	2	3	4	5	6	7	8	9	10	11
Fats, Oils & Sweets	1	2	3	4	5	6	7	8	9	10	
Water:	1	2	3	4	5	6	7	8	9	10	11

Today's Fitness (enter #'s and types that fit your daily routine):

_____ Reps of _____   _____ Reps of_____

_____ Reps of _____   _____ Reps of_____

_____ Reps of _____   _____ Reps of_____

Other:_____

Other:_____

Money I Spent Today:

$_____ for _____ In my budget?   Yes   No

$_____ for _____ In my budget?   Yes   No

$_____ for _____ In my budget?   Yes   No

Something I Cleaned today:_____

Positive Interactions today:_____

_____

What I did towards Spiritual Growth today:_____

Today my biggest Personal Success was:_____

What I did for Someone Else today:_____

Today I am Grateful for:_____

Today I Feel:_____

Today I Learned:_____

Today I treated myself with love and care: Yes   No

ONE DAY AT A TIME: A Self-Care Journal

One Day at a Time / A Self-Care Journal

54412879R00066

Made in the USA
Middletown, DE
04 December 2017